BREAKING **FREE**

Understanding
Sexual Addiction &
the Healing Power
of Jesus

Russell Willingham

InterVarsity Press
Downers Grove, Illinois

InterVarsity Press
P.O. Box 1400, Downers Grove, IL 60515
World Wide Web: www.ivpress.com
E-mail: mail@ivpress.com

InterVarsity Press® *is the book-publishing division of InterVarsity Christian Fellowship/USA*®*, a student movement active on campus at hundreds of universities, colleges and schools of nursing in the United States of America, and a member movement of the International Fellowship of Evangelical Students. For information about local and regional activities, write Public Relations Dept., InterVarsity Christian Fellowship/USA, 6400 Schroeder Rd., P.O. Box 7895, Madison, WI 53707-7895.*

All Scripture quotations, unless otherwise indicated, are taken from the Holy Bible, New International Version®*. NIV*®*. Copyright* ©*1973, 1978, 1984 by International Bible Society. Used by permission of Zondervan Publishing House. All rights reserved.*

The stories that appear in this book are based on the lives of real people. Names and details have been changed to protect the confidentiality of these individuals.

Cover illustration: Art Wolfe/Tony Stone Images

Illustrations on pp. 82, 83, 159: Roberta Polfus

ISBN 0-8308-1791-3

Printed in the United States of America ♾

Library of Congress Cataloging-in-Publication Data.

Willingham, Russell.
    Breaking free : understanding sexual addiction and the healing
power of Jesus / Russell Willingham.
    p. cm.
    Includes bibliographical references.
    ISBN 0-8308-1791-3 (paper : alk. paper)
    1. Sex addicts—Religious life. 2. Sex addiction—Religious
aspects—Christianity. 3. Sex addicts—Rehabilitation. 4. Sex
addiction—Treatment. I. Title.
BV4596.S42W55 1999
241'.66—dc21
                                                   98-54079
                                                      CIP

21	20	19	18	17	16	15	14	13	12	11	10	9	8	7	6	5	4
16	15	14	13	12	11	10	09	08	07	06	05	04	03	02	01		

To Keri.
We have both struggled,
but you paid the greater price.
You stood by me and gave me time to grow up.
Though I knew I had found a treasure
the first time I laid eyes on you—
fifteen years of marriage have only confirmed this.
I love you.

Contents

Acknowledgments

I would like to thank the many people God has used to impact my life. They have contributed to this book either directly or indirectly. Thank you, Trip Kimball, Roger Whitlow, Eric Nelson and Scott Falk, for pastoring and supporting me when lesser men would have kept their distance. Thank you, Bud Searcy, executive director of New Creation Ministries, for being my brother, mentor, friend and boss. Your life and teaching have shaped me more than you know. Thank you, Donna René Hopkins, my co-worker, for being the best friend and "little sister" a guy could have.

Thank you, Bob Davies, president of Exodus International, for greatly encouraging a first-time author and giving me practical guidance. To Mona Gansberg Hodgson and Virginia Muir for your editing expertise and invaluable suggestions. To Linda Doll at InterVarsity Press, who was the first to champion the book and see it through to its completion.

Thank you, Nick Ballew and Brian Nagel, for your love, friendship and support over the years. Thank you, Diane Ashmore, for knowing how to listen, how to speak and how to love. Thanks to all of the staff, leaders, board members and volunteers at New Creation Ministries for your hard work and encouragement. And, most of all, thank you to the men and women who have allowed me to tell your stories. I have been touched by your brokenness and courage.

Finally, thank you, Lord Jesus. You have kept every one of your promises and blessed me beyond my imagination. For any fruit that comes from this book I give you the credit. For any errors I take the blame.

Foreword

All the surveys I've read show the same thing: Huge numbers of Christian men—even leaders—are struggling with various forms of sexual addiction. And, until recently, there were few resources to point the way out. Fortunately, this lack of help is now changing, and this book is an important contribution to the literature on this subject.

Russell Willingham is my favorite type of writer. He doesn't just point the way in an abstract, detached manner. Rather, he invites you to come along on a mutual journey of discovery, as he tells you the details of his own struggle and how God has turned him from a defeated victim into a triumphant overcomer. You will be fascinated to read about his life, and you will be filled with hope for your own struggles. Russell has also worked with many men dealing with similar issues, and he shares insights from his counseling sessions with numerous clients.

Whether you are struggling with sexual addiction or know of someone who is, this practical book will give you effective answers. After examining the dynamics of how we get trapped in sexual addiction, Russell shows us the way out through allowing God to heal the underlying root issues and finding accountability with other believers.

The pathway to freedom is not easy. Along the way we must examine family dynamics, look at the biblical basis for our true identity and wrestle with the implications of our "dark side" of sin and shame. We must take an honest look at our inner loneliness, then bring God into our areas of deepest need. Finally, we must be committed to lives of rigorous honesty.

The solutions in this book are not simple, but they are effective. They have been tested in the lives of other men before being offered here. I am convinced that after reading this book you'll have the insights and practical tools to begin experiencing a whole new level of freedom.

It's my pleasure to recommend this volume to anyone who has felt hopeless, trapped and condemned by sexual addiction. You are holding the key to your freedom. Unlock it by absorbing and practicing the truths presented in this—and may God bless you with the same joy and liberty that he has brought into the lives of the author and many of the other men that you'll meet in these pages.

Bob Davies
Executive Director
Exodus International North America

Introduction

Lonely to the Core

I see men and women every day who struggle with sexual issues. They are all in pain. They are frustrated and confused by behavior they don't understand. They are construction workers, administrators, laborers, pastors, salesmen, police officers, homemakers and missionaries; and they are all Christians.

What makes people who love God indulge regularly in sexual sin? Is it a lack of commitment? A lack of will power? Perhaps they are not really saved at all? Most of us are quick to diagnose their problem and offer a solution. But my experience has shown me that a common thread runs through their lives—they are lonely to the core. That loneliness has not responded to increased church attendance, more intense Bible study or rebuking the devil. It seems to hang on and claw at their insides until they find themselves doing the very things they vowed they would never do.

My heart has ached as I have listened to their stories. I've also been angered by the ways they have wounded their families. Nevertheless, I have seen that these are people who genuinely care about morality but find themselves failing to live up to those moral principles. They have found little encouragement in the "quick fix" mentality of the Christians around them. Some of them, in a last-ditch attempt to find help before they abandon Christianity altogether, have come to us. Some of these same men and women are now finding freedom for the first time in their lives.

I listen to them in individual counseling as they tell me how God is beginning to put their lives back together again. I meet with them in groups and watch them minister to one another with an honesty and a love that I can only describe as breathtaking. Their wives have come to me and said, "I never thought I'd see the day when he would . . ." and they have continued with some report about renewed affection, honesty or intimacy that exceeds what they experienced even prior to the crisis. Not all their stories have a happy ending, however, because in the real world people fail. Some lose their families, their jobs or even their lives. We would like to think that for Christians it all works out in the end, but reality can be a bitter pill to swallow. Nevertheless, many of them are experiencing healing, one difficult inch at a time.

I first became interested in the work of New Creation Ministries after getting to know the executive director, Bud Searcy. As he shared with me what God was doing in the lives of sexually broken people, my heart thrilled. I could relate to the victories and defeats he described, because my wife and I had just come through our own "baptism of fire." My own sexually addictive behavior had taken its toll on our relationship.

Though I never strayed outside the marriage, my unresolved issues had caused me to have such unrealistic expectations about sex that it nearly pushed our relationship to the breaking point. A dozen years of in-depth Bible study, serious prayer and fruitful ministry had failed to eradicate this problem from my life. As we sought help, and as I began to understand how to let Jesus into that broken area of my heart, we began to mend. It was only natural for me to begin assisting Bud in the work that he and others were doing. When I saw how the Lord was transforming lives—in a way I had only dreamed about as a pastor—I was hooked. I have been on staff ever since.

In this book I will share with you what I am learning. I will show how the popular Christian culture has blinded us to the many priceless gems that Scripture contains. I will also draw from information that some might consider secular. I will offer twelve "essentials" I have found to be mandatory if someone is to undergo genuine transformation. This may frustrate those who want a more simplified approach to change, but I haven't found change to be that simple, either in my life or in the lives of those with whom I work. I have found it to be a messy and difficult process requiring patience and discernment as a variety of biblical truths are applied to it simultaneously.

As I describe the world of sexual addiction, I will not beat around the bush. I will try to be considerate of the sensibilities of the reader, but I must be honest about what goes on in the hearts of Christians who struggle in this area. We have nothing to fear from the truth. Why should Planned Parenthood be the only group giving out direct information on the subject of sex? (Some of theirs is erroneous, to be sure, but direct, nonetheless.) We will all benefit from a frank discussion of the problem and the solution.

The stories that appear in this book are based on the lives of real people. Names and details have been changed to protect the confidentiality of these individuals.

Finally, allow me to say that I don't believe in coincidence. You picked up this book for a reason. Someone you love may need the information contained here. Or the one who needs it may be you. The bitter struggles and hard-won victories of a number of people are described in the pages ahead. They are Christian believers, yet they have not been immune to addiction. The essentials of their recovery from sexually compulsive behavior are outlined in the clearest words I know how to use. These essentials are gleaned from my own experience and the experience of others who have found nothing else to be effective.

Jesus Christ is moving among his people as Savior and Healer. He said this about what the Father sent him to do:

He has sent me to bind up the brokenhearted,
    to proclaim freedom for the captives
    and release from darkness for the prisoners,
to proclaim the year of the LORD's favor
    and the day of vengeance of our God,

to comfort all who mourn,
   and provide for those who grieve in Zion—
to bestow on them a crown of beauty
   instead of ashes,
the oil of gladness
   instead of mourning,
and a garment of praise
   instead of a spirit of despair.
They will be called oaks of righteousness,
   a planting of the LORD
   for the display of his splendor. (Is 61:1-3)

If you want to see how the Son of God heals the sexually broken, come with me. He has been doing it for a long time, and he is very good at it. He invites you to accompany him as he steps into the world of those who are lonely to the core. Who knows, you may find to your surprise that the one breaking free is you.

1

What
We Are
Dealing
With

"How Do
I Know
If I'm Addicted?"

I sat down on a pile of wood and looked around. I often came here to think, next to this railroad track, because it was one of the few places I could find some privacy. *Father, I don't know what to do,* I prayed. *I've never felt this much pain, and I thought when I got married it would go away!*

Keri and I had been married for seven years. I loved her, but I felt as though she was indifferent to my needs. Every time I tried to tell her how lonely I was, she became defensive. It was becoming clear to me that our relationship was at a crossroads. *Father, I don't know whether she can't see my pain or whether she does see it but won't respond.* My feelings of rejection were overwhelming.

This was not a new experience for me. After my parents divorced, my mother turned to alcohol. She could never connect with me because of her drinking and constant relationships with a steady stream of violent, abusive men. In desperation I turned to the thing she seemed to be turning to—sex. As a seven-year-old I became sexual with every girl in the neighborhood who would have me. I devoured every page of pornography I happened to find in a field or on the roadside. Romance with a girl—any girl—became my constant, waking preoccupation.

In my teens I became even more dependent on porn. I would go into run-down used bookstores seeking it or to the "respectable" stores and stand for hours flipping through their sex manuals. I began taking increasingly greater risks and not caring who saw me. I looked through other people's windows when I thought there was a chance of seeing something. And I was not above homosexuality. By the time I was sixteen, I was masturbating once or twice a day and planning, with a friend of mine, to seek out a prostitute. I was blindly moving toward a cliff, not realizing the danger.

It was in this world of ever-increasing darkness that Jesus Christ found me. When I understood that all the truth I had been searching for was contained in him, I promptly abandoned my self-made New Age religion (I had picked that up along with all the sexual perversion) and made a full surrender to him. It was not long before I found a solid evangelical church and began growing rapidly. I dug deep into the Word and began cultivating a passionate prayer life. My habitual use of pornography and masturbation stopped. I attacked my stubborn tendency toward sexual fantasizing with a vengeance. I was moving forward and getting free of my previous life. Nevertheless, just below the surface the deep ache persisted. I had knocked all the branches off the twisted tree of my past—but the trunk, with all its roots, was still very much alive.

That is when I came to a brilliant conclusion: *I need to get married!* After all, didn't Paul say it was better to marry than to burn? A short time later I met Keri. She was short and had beautiful black hair. We fell in love and married nine months later. The first couple of years were incredible. I felt greatly loved by this woman, and we had sex often. But then the pain deep in my heart started moving to the surface. When it did, I would blame her for not "being there" for me. We would argue. There would be silence and hurt on both sides and then apologies all around. We would make up and be fine for another six months, when it all came up again.

This pattern went on for years. In the meantime we had a child, I entered the ministry and we moved three hundred miles from our hometown. It was at this point that the loneliness and despair caught up to me. That is when I ended up at the railroad tracks, pouring my heart out to God. I was so desperate I was even open to counseling. One thing led to another, and Keri and I ended up in the office of a therapist. She was a Christian, but I still felt uncomfortable seeing someone who had received "secular" training.

Opening up about what was really going on was not easy. It was, however, a major turning point in my life—not because our counselor gave such profound guidance (she mostly listened) but because the Lord himself began to fill in the blanks as I exposed my inner self to another believer. I had no idea that this was the biblical mode of healing (see Jas 5:16). I just did it because my other options had run out.

The Walking Wounded

My gradual restoration (as described later in this book) opened up a whole new world of ministry. I began volunteering, and then working full time, with New Creation Ministries. As someone on staff with an organization that specializes in helping the sexually broken, I have been exposed to an invisible subgroup within the church. These men and women are the walking wounded of the body of Christ. And they all have one thing in common: They have experienced abandonment. They were not necessarily left on someone's doorstep, but in key areas of their lives they have been forsaken. Many of them came from Christian homes where their parents did the best they could. Unfortunately, many of those parents had not been properly nurtured in *their* formative years either. Consequently, they could only give what they had received. In many cases it was not much.

John

John was a full-time Christian worker. He traveled and did evangelistic work in the churches within his denomination. He was articulate and theologically astute. I was impressed with him during our first appointment.

He came to see me because his wife had found out about his affairs and X-rated videos. She smashed the VCR on the back porch and told him to get help. After getting the particulars, I asked about his family.

"Well, I'm not sure what *that* has to do with anything," John said, "but

I came from a good Christian home. My parents had us in church every week, and we took Scripture very seriously. I believe it was my upbringing that influenced me to go into the ministry."

"How did your parents express affection to you?"

"My mother was very affectionate, but my dad was emotionally unavailable."

"How did that make you feel?"

"It made me feel rejected," he said, as his head drooped.

"What kind of relationship do you have with your dad now?"

"It's getting better. When I was about forty, he finally told me he loved me. That felt really good."

"I get the impression that you wanted to hear it sooner."

"Yeah, I did. I never felt like I measured up. I couldn't understand what I had done to make him not want to be involved with me."

"Perhaps that's just where *he* was. Maybe it wasn't about you at all."

"You could be right. But I've struggled with insecurity all my life as a result."

"Could it be that your womanizing and compulsive 'need' to use videos is an attempt to get some kind of nurturing?"

John began to see that his problem wasn't only about sex. It was about legitimate, unmet needs. Did that mean that his sexual behavior was therefore acceptable? Not at all. This man was involved in serious sin, but sin was not the *only* thing we were dealing with. And since every pastor or counselor he had seen dealt with it at the sin level only, the changes never lasted.

Sexual Problem or Sexual Addiction?

Not everyone who struggles with a sexual problem is dealing with an addiction. Dr. Archibald Hart, in his excellent book *The Sexual Man,* found that the vast majority of godly Christian men in his survey were deeply troubled by the intensity of their sexual feelings.[1]

Some of what passes for lust is testosterone, not moral weakness. Are men, therefore, not responsible to rein it in? Of course they are. Matthew 5:28 says, "Anyone who looks at a woman lustfully has already committed adultery with her in his heart." What the Lord *didn't* say was, "If you see a beautiful woman and feel an inward pull—you've sinned!"

In other words, simply noticing an attractive woman and responding emotionally is not lust. It's that second look, taken with the intention of mental pursuit, that is adulterous. The King James Version (which is closer to the original Greek in this instance) makes this meaning even clearer: "Whosoever looketh on a woman to lust after her hath committed adultery with her already in his heart." Picture a person driving around town running errands. He has been too busy to notice that it's past lunchtime. What happens when he approaches a fast-food place and his senses are overwhelmed by the smell of burgers and fries? The reaction is immediate and involuntary. His stomach growls, he salivates and swallows, and a sense of weakness washes over him. He may turn in, or he may drive past, but he has no control over what happens inside of his body at that moment. What he *can* control is how he responds to it.

Though sexual desire (unlike food) is not a matter of survival, it is tied to deep needs for love that are a matter of survival. To feel shame and guilt about an initial attraction makes as much sense as condemning yoiurself for hunger at one o'clock in the afternoon. It's how you handle that initial attraction and where you go with it that decides the morality of your choice.

This is a fine line we're talking about, but a distinction that needs to be made. A lot of men are walking around feeling guilt simply for being sexual. I think of several reasons for this:

☐ Many Christians are not honest with each other about the degree of sexual arousal they experience. Consequently, when one man experiences a high sex drive, he thinks he is the only one.

☐ Some Christian parents discuss sex with their sons in an awkward or halting way, giving the impression that they are ashamed or uncomfortable, passing that ambience on to them. In other homes it isn't discussed at all. This also makes a statement.

☐ A common perception in our society is that all men are "sex maniacs." Often our wives reinforce this feeling of shame. "What? You want it again tonight?!" Husbands then get the impression that something must be wrong with them for being such "animals."

☐ Many forget that an entire book of the Bible is devoted to sexual love—the Song of Solomon. The Scriptures also contain robust statements like this: "May your fountain be blessed, and may you rejoice in the wife of your youth. A loving doe, a graceful deer—may her breasts satisfy you always, may you ever be captivated by her love" (Prov 5:18-19).

☐ Many have failed in the area of lust so often that they mistakenly think *all* sexual feelings are in the same category.

Lots of men feel uncomfortable with their sexuality for these reasons. These are not signs, however, of a sexual addiction. Christian men, in their attempt to follow the Lord, will struggle with these issues from time to time. But, as we shall see, the sexual addict has this and a lot more on his plate.

Signs of Sexual Addiction

Below is a list of characteristics that accompany abnormal behavior. I have found them to be accurate signs of sexual addiction as well:

1. Age-inappropriate behavior
2. Intense reactions in response to minimal stress
3. Frequency of symptoms
4. Degree of social disruption produced by symptoms
5. Inner suffering
6. Rigidity and persistence of the symptoms
7. Physical damage[2]

Age-inappropriate behavior. This may not be related directly to sexuality, but I have observed it in the life of every sex addict I have ever counseled. It is what some have called "arrested development." For example, a thirty-year-old man may act like a six-year-old. He says to himself, *That's just the way I am,* but everyone around him can see how childish his behavior is. When others try to point this out, he becomes defensive and thinks everyone is just being critical.

At a time in his life when he should be able to think about the needs of others, he is often stuck in a selfish mode. His dealings with his wife are characterized by insensitivity. He will come home late and not bother to call and let her know his plans. He may insist on sex at the drop of a hat or ignore her sexual needs altogether.

His children often take a back seat to the TV, newspaper, gym or ministry. When he does attempt to spend "quality time" with them, it is usually brief and superficial (unless it involves an activity that *he* likes—then he can do it for hours, giving the impression that he is a devoted father).

This kind of selfishness is obvious, but another side of his narcissism is harder to spot: He can be giving, complimentary, pleasant and positive around everyone outside of the family, and they may think of him as "Mr. Personality." But these can all be unconscious attempts to manipulate them into meeting his hunger for approval. He is a needy little boy in an adult body.

Intense reactions in response to minimal stress. When the sex addict does not get his way—look out! He will explode, withdraw or manipulate. One of the areas where this can typically be seen is in his sexual relationship with his wife. If she declines his advances, he may lie in bed staring at the ceiling and heaving deep sighs. Or he may go sleep on the couch as a demonstration of his passive rage.

If he is the more aggressive type, he launches into a tirade about how "you never meet my needs." This guilt-inducing tactic is usually effective for a few years. But eventually his wife will see through it and will no longer buy into it. As childish as all of this may seem, his feelings of rejection are profoundly real. This doesn't mean that his wife really is rejecting him, but he *perceives* it that way.

The sense of rejection is followed by feelings of hopelessness and despair that may last for days. At this point he will resort to masturbation, pornography or another relationship. He feels that since his wife said no to sex she was, in fact, despising him as a person. This reaction betrays a deep level of childhood brokenness that he mistakenly thinks a loving wife or a sexual fix can address.

Frequency of symptoms. Even the most secure spouse will occasionally feel put off by the other's sexual disinterest. But, as we have demonstrated, the sexually broken man will consistently respond this way. And though most men have a fairly high sex drive, the addicted man is obsessed in this area. For him *everything* contains sexual innuendo. The way women dress, smell, talk, cry or worship is a turn-on to him.

Along with the internal symptoms, the external behaviors are frequent as well. For instance, not every man who has an affair is a sex addict, as tragic as even one affair is. It is the frequency of the affairs or the frequency of fantasizing about one that shows an addictive problem. A man who masturbates two or three times a year is not necessarily an addict (though he might be defrauding his wife or engaging in lust), but daily or weekly masturbation could be a sign of addiction.

Though even a single exposure to pornographic magazines or videos is destructive to a person's spiritual life, it is the frequency of their use that determines whether an addiction is present. This distinction is an important one; while the occasional slip in one of these areas can be overcome by renewed discipline and vigilance, sexual addiction can be overcome only by more drastic measures.

Degree of social disruption produced by symptoms. All of us have sexual difficulties at one time or another, but for the addict these difficulties place an incredible strain on relationships. The first person it affects, obviously, is the spouse. I have heard some wives say, "I wish he *would* go out and have an affair so he could stop bothering me about sex!" I've watched other women, who were less sure of themselves, begin to question their worth as persons because their husbands wanted constant sex or none at all.

The disruption also affects the children. This is something the addict usually doesn't think about. The children notice the tension between Dad and Mom, and though they may not say anything, their insecurities grow as the tension escalates. Many children rush in to provide some kind of relief by cracking a joke to break the tension, by being the "perfect child" so the family will have a reason to stay together, or by getting into trouble themselves, thereby diverting the tension from husband-wife to parent-child. Children adopt these roles (Mascot, Perfect Child, Scapegoat and so on) in an attempt to bring stability to the family. Unfortunately, they sacrifice their childhood in the process.

Job performance suffers as well. The addicted man may be late to work because of cruising for prostitutes or stopping to look at magazines. He may take "breaks" in order to masturbate in the bathroom or car. He may flirt with, sexually harass or have affairs with female co-workers. Needless to say, none of these things makes for a pleasant or productive work environment.

Prostitution, voyeurism (looking through people's windows), exhibitionism, rape and child molestation are examples of illegal behavior that some addicts use to meet their need. We may think that Christians could never be involved in such things. But Scripture has at least one account of a man of God manipulating the people around him and breaking the law in an attempt to satisfy his sexual urges. Not only did he use his position of power to get sex, he also used a member of his staff to cover his tracks by arranging a murder (2 Sam 11). Though David may not have been a sex addict, this incident certainly produced the social disruption common to sexual addiction.

Inner suffering. The loneliness inside the sexually broken man is horrific. It is so unbearable for him that when it rises up, he feels the need to silence it immediately with some kind of sexual act. He believes that if he allowed it to come to the top, he would die. A pastor in my group for Christian leaders felt this pain so acutely that he drove to a remote area and parked by a railroad track. He sat there for hours, waiting for the train—fully intending to jump in front of it when it arrived. It was during the wait that he decided to contact us. (Thank God for late trains!)

The addict believes, deep down, that he is not worth loving in the first place. This is the reason for his loneliness. The addict has already *assumed* he is unlovable, so he consistently deflects the affection expressed to him by others. This, of course, becomes a self-fulfilling prophecy. Eventually they stop reaching out and pull away from him altogether.

Some addicts still relate to others but only in a way that doesn't risk their inner core. Others choose not to relate to people at all but find it easier to relate to a thing (a magazine, piece of clothing or fetish). In time, the pornographic fantasy becomes more satisfying than real relationships with all their demands, challenges and possibilities for rejection.

The inner suffering of the sex addict comes from two sources: deep, unmet emotional needs from childhood and the pain and disappointment caused by trying to meet those needs through his sinful behavior. Psychology in its worst form focuses on the pain and does not believe in the existence of sin. Christianity in its worst form focuses exclusively on the sin and considers the pain irrelevant. Neither approach is helpful; each is damaging.

The addict is constantly wondering, *Is everybody this lonely inside?* The person who has had his basic need for love and nurturing met has a hard time even conceiving of the inner pain that the sexual addict lives with every day.

Rigidity and persistence of the symptoms. A true addict is someone who has attempted many times to stop, but without success. He has a paradoxical love of acting out sexually and, at the same time, a bitter hatred of it. Some are able to stop for years at a time, but then the longings resurface with a vengeance and the behavior resumes. (This is often true of newly married sex addicts who think marriage will "cure" them.)

One youth minister said, "I pleaded and prayed to God hundreds of times but with little long-term effect. The question I kept coming back to was: How can this be? I am a Christian, I love my wife, I have two special kids and I am a minister—what is wrong with me?"

One reason Christians are so stumped by this problem is the one-sided view they take of it. They see it primarily as a moral issue, and since many of them are very moral, they don't understand how they can continue to violate their own deeply held convictions. What they fail to grasp is that sexual addiction is not only about sin, it is also about real need.

The addict's need is not for sex (though he *thinks* it is); his need is for love. If that need goes unmet, he will live in a perpetual state of "hunger," looking for something to satisfy it. Even if he discontinues his sexual behavior for a while, his underlying yearning for love will not be addressed. Soon he finds his good intentions being overwhelmed by a longing that won't go away.

Physical damage. Addicts who do not experience healing will eventually experience some kind of physical damage. Some have injured themselves directly through their sexual behavior or have suffered the effects of disease and infection. Several people in our ministry have died of AIDS.

The most common physical damage is not a direct result of the sexual acting out. It is a result of other ways in which the deeper issues come out. A majority of sex addicts deal with other compulsive behaviors as well: eating disorders, workaholism, spending problems, substance abuse or frantic religious activity (mistakenly called "ministry"). Many experience obesity, high blood pressure, pain in their joints, anxiety and panic attacks, severe mood swings, depression, fatigue, sleeping disorders, extreme irritability or any of a host of other physical and emotional maladies.

They may experience physical damage to their property or possessions as a result of being involved in risky sexual behavior: being beaten while "cruising" in a park looking for sexual contacts; having jilted lovers break windows in their home or car; paying out thousands of dollars they can't afford on phone sex, prostitution, legal fees or fines. Few sex addicts experience all of these problems, but any degree of identification with this list should cause great concern.

Sexual Addiction Defined

Here is a long definition with several important parts, each of which we will discuss.

> Sexual addiction is an obsessive-compulsive relationship with a person, object or experience for the purpose of sexual gratification. Whatever the type or amount of the behavior, it is damaging spiritually, physically or both. The addict has repeatedly tried to stop the behavior but at the same time is terrified of stopping. What drives the addiction is inadequate spirituality and deep unmet childhood needs that are valid but are mistakenly thought to be sexual needs. The behavior usually starts in pre-adolescence and tends to shape the orientation and personality of the individual. Genuine recovery is possible only with outside intervention and divine help.

Addiction is an obsessive-compulsive relationship. Some addicts think about sex literally all the time, but this is not true of all. The addict can be involved in other activities for a while, but he tends to return to his obsessive "core" in a few hours or days. He is like the bird who flies far and wide and does all kinds of things but always returns to the nest. For the addict, sexual thoughts and fulfillment are the "nest."

All men can be sexually compulsive from time to time, but for the addict this compulsion is the bedrock from which many of his decisions, plans, motives, thoughts and actions unconsciously spring. He finds himself acting out sexually and then saying, *How did I get here? I've got to stop this,* only to find himself in the same situation a short time later. He can really identify with the words of Paul, "For what I do is not the good I want to do; no, the evil I do not want to do—this I keep on doing" (Rom 7:19).

The addict may say that Jesus is the most important person in his life, but when the chips are down, it isn't *Jesus* to whom he runs—it's the addiction. He is addicted to the mood-altering experience of sex (the "high" just before and during acting out). He may be attached to an object—women's undergarments, for example. The object itself brings a feeling of security and arousal—a real person isn't needed. Or he may be addicted to a person. This person may be a favorite prostitute, a lover or even his wife.

Strange as it may sound, a person can be attached to his spouse in a way that is very unhealthy. What passes for love in many Christian marriages is actually a very needy, dependent and dysfunctional way of using the spouse to meet needs he or she was never intended to meet.

Whatever the addictive behavior, it is damaging spiritually. We've already talked about physical damage to self, family and property, but what about spiritual damage? This is the most tragic loss of all. Sexual addiction is an idolatrous attempt to meet our need apart from God:

> My people have committed two sins:
> They have forsaken me,
>   the spring of living water,
> and have dug their own cisterns,
>   broken cisterns that cannot hold water. (Jer 2:13)

The Holy Spirit says some surprising things here. First, he says the ones who are doing this are *his people.* That should forever settle the question, "Can Christians be involved in idolatry?" The next thing he says is that his people have forsaken him. Sexual addiction is not just a matter of having a bad habit or weakness—it is an *abandonment* of God.

Next, God says that instead of drinking from the ever-flowing stream, we have gone out and created our own inadequate ways of satisfying our thirst. The problem is, we were not meant to kneel at the bottom of this self-made cistern and ingest handfuls of dirt. We were meant to drink from the fresh, satisfying waters of the living stream. By his behavior the sex addict is saying, "Lord, I don't believe you can meet this need, and I never have. So I'm going to meet it *my* way."

Another thing the Spirit says in this verse is, "Your longing is valid—it's where you're going with it that is not." God does not condemn our legitimate thirst for love, including erotic love. However, what the addict calls sexual desire is actually a mixture of unmet childhood needs, a hunger for God, legitimate arousal, conditioned electrochemical responses in the brain and lust—all in one package. He mistakenly thinks that one sex act will address all of these needs!

The addict does not bring his *true self* into the sexual act. The true self has already been deeply wounded, so he refuses to expose it to further rejection. He would rather engage in the predictable ritual of sex than uncover his true self. This choice may protect him from endangering his soft inner core, but it also ensures that the needs of that core never get met. Consequently, he uses objects, romance or a "special person" to take the edge off his loneliness without ever admitting how lonely he really is.

This is not to say that the sexually addicted Christian has no spiritual life. I have met sex addicts who were involved in fruitful missionary work, evangelism, teaching and leadership. But these activities *also* become a way of trying to meet their needs under the guise of ministry.

Some think that because they have intense times of worship, prayer or Bible study, they are relating deeply to God. But genuine intimacy with God is a long, grueling process that involves being stripped of our attachments and false securities to stand naked before him. This the addict will not tolerate. So he finds himself between a rock and a hard place: he longs for God to free him, but he is terrified of life without the addiction. He is split against himself and rendered spiritually unstable (see Jas 1:7). This creates great spiritual damage to his soul.

The person has repeatedly attempted to stop. The Christians I've worked with have repeatedly tried to stop their behavior but without success. It isn't until they experience spectacular failure or simply grow tired of their chronic compulsion that they finally reach out for help.

This reaching out for help is the *first* step toward healing, not the last-ditch attempt that most of them think it is. The fear and spiritual pride of addicted people are awesome. They desperately want to believe they are in control, and they try to convince others that they are. They suffer a terrible blow to their ego when they have to admit that sin really is as powerful as the Bible says it is.

Two things drive the addiction. I have said that two things are the driving force of sexual addiction: An inadequate spirituality and unmet childhood needs. First, let's look at spirituality. The Christian addict may have allowed Jesus into every area of his heart with which he is *consciously* in touch. But he reserves entire regions of his spirit for the addiction.

Most strugglers do not believe, deep down, that God can touch this ache. If they are open to that possibility, however, they are then faced with a second question, "How do I let him into *this* part of my heart?" The answer to that is not simple. I will devote an entire chapter to it, but at this point I will say it involves what I call the Great Transference.

Jesus once talked with a woman who had a similar ache in her soul. In her attempt to address the ache, she had married five times. Finally she gave up on the institution of marriage and just moved in with guy number six. What did Jesus say to her? Did he advise her and her boyfriend to visit a sex therapist? Read more books on communication? No. He said, "If you knew the gift of God and who it is that asks you for a drink, you would have asked him and he would have given you living water" (Jn 4:10). He was challenging her to make the Great Transference from sex to him.

The fact that we're saved doesn't mean we are not still looking for Jesus. He may have come in, but we still have dry areas he needs to fill. We have to transfer those needs from the adult bookstore, bedroom and pages of *Hustler* to the place of prayer. Not only this, but some of the areas he needs to fill were intended to be filled by someone else at an earlier date. This brings us to the second force behind sexual addiction: unmet childhood needs.

Many Christians don't understand how profound their need is to receive nurturing and affirmation in childhood. As I counseled with one woman, I asked her to describe the relationship she had with her parents.

"What kind of personalities did your parents have?" I asked.

"Well, my mom was very controlling. She could be outspoken and rigid. I've always admired her convictions, but I wouldn't want to be like her."

"How about your dad?"

"I have a lot of respect for Dad. He was always quiet, and for years I thought it was because he was stupid or something. As I got older, I realized that he was actually very intelligent."

"You've described a family that was involved in lots of activities. Your mother was controlling and your father was passive. Am I getting this right?"

"Yeah."

"Do you understand that being active as a family is not the same as being nurtured by that family?"

Her eyebrows drew together. "Uh, I think so."

"Your mother can't control you and nurture you at the same time. And a passive father is unable to be assertive in the way that genuine nurturing requires."

I continued, "For all of the good things your family was involved in, your home life lacked genuine closeness, didn't it?"

Her eyes filled with tears. "Yes, it did."

"Is it such a mystery why you've thrown open the doors of your heart to a steady stream of men?"

"No, it isn't. I think I see what you're saying."

Our need for food, clothing and shelter can be met, but we can still experience profound problems if our basic need for nurturing is not satisfied. A study done by Dr. H. M. Skeels proved how true this is. She took thirteen children from an orphanage and placed them in a women's facility to be cared for by some of the inmates and staff. In this new setting the children were rocked, cuddled and lovingly spoken to—things the overcrowded orphanage could not provide.

In a two-and-a-half-year period the children's I.Q.s increased an average of twenty-nine points. The I.Q.s of the children in the original institution *dropped* twenty-six points during the same period! Dr. Skeels tracked both groups for thirty years and found that her subjects went on to integrate normally into society. Those in the original institution were never released, due to mental retardation and lack of social functioning (although one got a job as a dishwasher).

The point is clear: Nurturing is a matter of emotional life and death. That is why Paul said, "And, ye fathers, provoke not your children to wrath: but bring them up in the *nurture* and admonition of the Lord" (Eph

6:4 KJV). Many parents, including Christian parents, are great in the admonition department but drop the ball when it comes to nurturing. And, notice, this is not nurturing the way *we* think it ought to be done, but is the nurturing and admonition *of the Lord.* In other words, we are commanded to nurture as God nurtures.

Nurture is not a matter of teaching children to memorize Bible verses and go to Sunday school. It is a matter of affirming them and speaking words of life to their sense of self the way God does to us. Parenting requires an anointing of the Holy Spirit and a sensitivity to the heart of God that few parents have. Is it any wonder that this generation—even within the church—is so vulnerable to a variety of obsessive and compulsive behaviors?

The behavior starts in pre-adolescence. Most children experiment with sexual behavior—everything from playing doctor to "I'll show you mine if you show me yours." However, the child who later becomes a sexual addict tends to get involved in sexual behavior a good five years before the usual age. In *The Sexual Man,* Archibald Hart said his respondents recalled their first sexual feelings taking place around age 12.[3] The men I've worked with had strong sexual feelings as early as 8 to 10. His respondents stated that they first masturbated around the age of 13.[4] Those I have counseled began between the ages of 9 and 12. Hart's men recall being exposed to pornography around the age of 15.[5] Those I've seen are exposed during the 9 to 12 age range.

Do Dr. Hart's respondents have poor memories or problems telling the truth? I don't think so. These figures are reasonable for those coming out of fairly healthy homes. That is just it; sex addicts usually don't come from healthy homes. They come from families that have a difficult time providing real nurturing. As I've said, Christian families are not immune to this. Often our ideas as Christian parents are a lot closer to our next-door neighbor's than to God's. The only difference is that we quote Bible verses as we wound our child's spirit.

Am I saying that the sexual addict has nothing to do with the formation of his own addiction? Of course not. Though his pain from childhood is real, he is still responsible for the sexual way he manages it today.

Legalistic prohibitions may influence him to curtail the behavior, but they fail to address the emotional deficit behind that behavior. For this reason, the addict either takes up the behavior again (when he can no longer ignore the cry of his soul) or switches to some socially acceptable addiction like workaholism or eating. This is why understanding the root issues of sexual addiction is so important. If we can grasp when and where the holes in our hearts began to form, then we know what areas the Lord Jesus has to touch.

The behavior tends to shape the orientation and personality. Many believers who struggle with sexually compulsive behavior think it indicates an insincere faith. But let me ask a question: Is it realistic to assume that a twenty- or thirty-year-old man who has used pornography and masturbation since the age of eight is going to experience complete internal change just because he goes forward at an evangelistic crusade?

"God can do anything!" some might say. True enough. But many of us struggle with fears, jealousies and pride that we have had since childhood. We often extend compassion to those who struggle in *these* areas (since we can relate) but expect the sexual addict to change overnight.

The addict's coping mechanisms have become deeply ingrained as a result of his experiences in childhood and adolescence. That is why the man who has consumed porn or lived in the party scene for many of his pre-Christian years will, most likely, tend to view women as objects even if he has a genuine new birth. We can be thankful that such an orientation can change, but that change will require high accountability and a lot of determination.

Recovery is possible only with outside intervention. A genuine sex addict cannot experience healing in isolation. It is too cunning, powerful and baffling to handle alone. Not only that, but the addict is too practiced in his unique form of twisted logic to change without an outsider to point out his blind spots. Sexual addiction is about relational deficits from childhood. Those relational gaps from the past *must be filled in relational ways today* with members of the same sex.

Much of the love that the addict seeks from women can, in fact, be adequately supplied by men. I am not talking about homosexuality but about healthy and intimate relating to another brother. This is difficult for the addict to grasp, because he honestly believes that his need is for sex.

He doesn't realize that what he needs is love, and that love can come in surprising ways from other honest, gutsy men.

Recovery is possible only with divine help. The addict does not know how to let divine help touch his need in the sexual area. Many have found the twelve steps helpful in this regard. But the twelve steps, as good as they are, are limited in what they can do. Those who work the steps but do not move on to intimacy with God eventually experience frustration and partial recovery, not the full transformation that Jesus intended when he said, "I have come that they may have life, and have it to the full" (Jn 10:10).

Conclusion

We have seen how deep-seated sexual addiction can be. It is not just a matter of sin. It is a combination of spiritual, hormonal, environmental and volitional factors. This in no way absolves the addict of his responsibility, but it helps him understand some of the ways he got where he is. With that understanding he can begin clawing his way out, with God's help.

We have taken a brief look at the origins of sexual addiction and its definition. In chapter two we will examine its mechanics.

2

The Dynamics of Sexual Addiction

What All Addicts Have in Common

Despite different backgrounds and different patterns of expressing needs, everyone who struggles with sexual addiction has something in common with all other strugglers. Notice how the following men attempt to get their needs met.

Jim

Man, what a day! The phone never stopped ringing, and Jim felt as if he got nothing done all day. He couldn't wait for five o'clock to come. After stopping to get a magazine on the way home, he pulled into the driveway of his apartment. He felt excited as he unlocked the door.

After letting himself in, he headed for the couch. He knew that his roommate wouldn't be home for a couple of hours, so that gave him plenty of time. It took only a few pages before he found what he was looking for. *Man, is she gorgeous,* he thought.

As Jim masturbated, he fantasized about her. She came to life in the theater of his mind. Occasionally he peeked at the magazine to refresh the bold image then closed his eyes again. In a few moments it was over.

He basked in the warm glow for a moment—but then it returned: the emptiness. It felt horrible. He always forgot about how awful it felt "after." *Oh, God, why do I keep doing this? Please forgive me.* He knew it was wrong and it had to stop.

Grabbing the magazine, he walked out the back door and flung it into the dumpster. *That does it, Lord, I'm not going to do it anymore!* He was so glad that God understood and was quick to forgive. *I'm serious, Lord. From now on I'm going to serve you—and I'm going to keep away from porn.* Tragically, Jim really believed this.

Nathan

Nathan always enjoyed the time he spent with Kelly. At fifteen his daughter was pretty, intelligent and athletic. They would rent movies or go out to eat. Their relationship was good. Since the divorce, Nathan had worked hard to be a good father.

But he dreaded taking her home every Sunday afternoon. As he headed toward his ex-wife's house he thought to himself, *You wouldn't be doing this if you hadn't been such a jerk to Kelly's mother.* Nathan was not a Christian when he married Judy. And he didn't know the first thing about being a husband. Of course, Judy was no saint either, but Nathan admitted he was the main reason the marriage failed. Even after all these years, he still felt guilty.

Normally Nathan was fine being alone, but Sunday nights were the worst. The good times he and Kelly had together made the house feel that much emptier when she was gone.

After a kiss and a wave he dropped her off at the curb. Not wanting to go home, he headed for the West Side. He knew they'd be there. He found the street he was looking for and made a right. As he slowed down to cruising speed, he saw several of them walking down the sidewalk.

Two blocks away he spotted another one. She flashed a broad smile as he drove past. Nathan's heart began to race and he circled back around. When she spotted him again, she motioned for him to come over. He pulled to the curb and waited, listening to the sound of her high heels click-clacking on the sidewalk. She leaned into the open window and said, "Hey, baby, looking for a date?" They agreed on a price and she got into the car.

Once in the motel room he did the same thing he did with all the others. The ritual of it felt good and helped him forget. When it was over he wanted to leave as fast as he could.

In the parking lot he noticed a drug dealer standing on the corner and some dangerous-looking guys leaning on the wall only a few feet away. Why hadn't he seen them a few minutes ago? As he drove away he wondered, *Why am I here? I'm gonna get robbed or killed if I keep doing this.*

Bill

Bill ran and jumped on the train before it took off. Whew! That was close. He always took the train out of Beijing on Friday evenings so he could spend the weekends with his beloved Kim. It was a good thing his wife, Susan, didn't like traveling and encouraged him to go alone. Otherwise, she might want to come along and see this "missionary" work he did.

Bill *was* involved in missionary work. And God used him. But Bill also used his ministry as a way of making contact with needy women. He had met Kim while pioneering a work in King Mui village. She knew both English and Chinese and was helpful to him. Young, independent and eager to embrace Western ways, Kim had fallen right under his spell. Before long they fell desperately in love. Or was it obsession? Sometimes Bill wondered. All he knew was that he could not live without her.

As far as Bill was concerned, Susan only criticized him and refused to see his good qualities. In actuality, she was the only one who saw through his charming façade to the selfishness below. Bill sought women who could appreciate his unique "gifts."

In ten years Bill had been with eight Chinese women. Susan knew about only one of them, and she had forgiven him for that. But if she found out about the others, he was sure she would leave him and go back to America. He knew that if that ever happened, their supporters would find out and withdraw their financial support, and his missionary career would be over.

Roger

Why does she have to be so impossible? Roger wondered. *This woman really makes my blood boil!* Roger was feeling very tired after another of his world-class arguments with Pam. Pam was feeling the same way. In reality, for years neither of them had heard what the other was saying.

They fought about sex, kids and money. Mostly money. Roger was an attorney and Pam a physician. Roger's law practice had been losing clients, so he used more and more of his wife's money to bankroll his hobbies. He would fly to Las Vegas on the spur of the moment just to have fun. Or he would do things like come home with a brand new computer system. When Pam would ask, "Where did you get the money for that?" Roger would say not to worry, that he would pay her back. But he never did.

Roger liked action movies, especially if they showed some skin. When the steamy parts came on, he would take in every fleshly detail. From time to time, he also rented movies that were obviously focused on sex. Since they were R-rated and not "triple X" (he would never rent *that* stuff!) he felt justified.

Scenes from these videos would play in his mind for weeks. He would also add details of his own. More and more often his stepdaughter became a character in these fantasies. Stephanie was Pam's daughter from a previous marriage. She had been eight years old when he and Pam met. Now she was sixteen. Stephanie liked wearing skimpy clothes during the day and revealing nightshirts before bedtime. The trap was being set by the devil.

When thoughts about Stephanie first began, Roger was horrified. He resisted them and prayed for forgiveness. But times had changed. Roger was not praying much anymore. He wasn't reading his Bible either. The family belonged to a big church that made it easy to remain anonymous. Their church attendance was the last vestige of Christianity they had left. The family was, in fact, losing its soul.

One night Roger was home with the kids while Pam worked at the hospital. As he went upstairs to turn in for the night, he noticed that Stephanie's bedroom door was ajar. Crazy thoughts began to fill his mind. For just a moment he hesitated, then he decided to go and "check on her."

He walked quietly down the hall and slowly pushed open the door. She was asleep. He watched her for a moment. She was so pretty, almost a woman. He crept up to her bedside and stared down at her. His heart was pounding so hard now that his breathing was labored.

He bent down and kissed her on the cheek. She stirred but then became still again. He felt a hunger inside that was so deep it moved his hands. He began to touch her body. Pleasure and terror filled his brain at the same time. After he touched her between the legs, she rolled over. Roger pulled his hands back, and it hit him. *My God, what am I doing?* He got off his knees and walked out.

He felt numb as he went into his room and sat on the bed. For a long, long time he just stared at the wall. *What's wrong with me?* he wondered. *I've just molested my stepdaughter!* He wanted to cry out for mercy, but he was sure that God would have nothing to do with him.

I'll never do that again, he reassured himself. *Thank God she was asleep.* What Roger didn't know was that Stephanie had been awakened by his kiss. After that, her fear prompted her to pretend to be asleep. The next day Child Protective Services was notified.

Sam

Sam worked full time as an office manager and part time as a pastor. The people in his congregation saw him as an anointed preacher. Those at the office saw him as a great guy who did his job well (though they felt he went a little overboard on the "religion thing").

His wife, Nicole, respected his understanding of the Word and took a lot of pride in being married to "Pastor Sam." People in the church would often say things like "You must be blessed to be the wife of such a wonderful man!" Nicole would nod her head and smile in agreement, but in private she resented her husband because of his constant preoccupation with sex.

Sam had always been that way. He had used pornography before he was saved. But God had "delivered him" from that and he never looked back. He didn't need to—he had Nicole. She was his living centerfold. Even if she had a raging vaginal infection, he would still insist on sex. Several times over the years this kind of "lovemaking" necessitated trips to the emergency room.

No matter what she did, it never seemed enough for Sam. Her self-esteem began to crumble, and she started questioning her faith. Didn't the Bible say that her body belonged to her husband, as Sam frequently reminded her? Did God really want her to live this way? If so, she wasn't sure how much longer she could hold out.

She felt something was wrong with Sam. But everyone's constant praise of him made her think *she* was the crazy one. In reality, Sam was a sex addict. But since he no longer used pornography or masturbation, he felt he was perfectly normal. All he needed, in his mind, was a wife who would "loosen up a bit." Sam didn't know it, but he was using his wife to meet needs that were not sexual at all. The marriage was in deep trouble.

The Cycle of Addiction

These men are all sex addicts. Though their addiction expresses itself in different ways, they share common characteristics. These characteristics form a cycle of addiction.

I am indebted to Stephen Arterburn's breakdown of this cycle in his book *Addicted to Love*. His remarks form the basis of this section. I have expanded it in a way that I believe will be helpful.

In every case, unmet needs lead to the following steps which form a pattern that is strengthened by repetition.

1. Visual/emotional trigger
2. Repression of pain with immediate sexual/romantic longings
3. Fantasizing/planning stage
4. The hunt
5. The connection
6. The act
7. Fulfillment
8. The letdown
9. The vow
10. The cycle resumes[1]

1. Visual/emotional trigger. The visual trigger can be anything that has a sexual connotation. Some obvious examples would be women on billboards, on TV or in magazines. The trigger can be the sound of a woman's voice or the sight of any woman, anywhere, who is the least bit attractive.

For the sex addict the visual stimulation triggers a painful awareness of need. The presence of an attractive woman (either real or symbolized) is enough to remind him of his unmet nurturing need. Though it is based on a legitimate deficit, it expresses itself as lust.

The emotional trigger is also activated when he is insulted, rejected or ignored. The addict has trained himself to run to something sexual when he has any negative emotion. This brings us to the second stage of the cycle.

2. *Repression of pain with immediate sexual/romantic longings.* The addict doesn't have to be sexual in order to find some relief. The *anticipation* of a sexual experience is enough to get him by for awhile. Remember how Jim felt better the moment he took his mind off his troubles and began anticipating the satisfaction ahead? Nathan did the same thing right after he dropped off his daughter. When the car pulled away from the curb, he was already repressing his loneliness and making plans to find a prostitute. Many addicts have been making this substitution for so long that they don't realize it is happening until they are well into the cycle.

Most addicts are taught as children that certain emotions are "bad" (anger and fear, for instance). Consequently, as adults they feel an urgency to get rid of such feelings as soon as they appear. The addict uses fantasizing and sex to accomplish this.

Unfortunately, he also feels a lot of shame about his sexuality. To admit to himself that he is "horny" is tantamount, in his mind, to saying he is evil, unspiritual or perverted. Though he may say sex is God's good gift, deep in his heart he feels guilty for enjoying it.

3. *Fantasizing/planning stage.* After the addict has repressed his pain with thoughts of sex, he moves into active fantasizing or planning. Now he is not dealing with a momentary thought of sexual fulfillment—he is savoring every detail.

For Jim this phase would last as many hours as it took to go from a stressful environment to his couch or bed. For Bill, the missionary, this phase lasted weeks or months. He would meet a woman and become obsessed with her. He would fantasize about her often and plan ways to win her over. Every word, gesture or smile became the execution of a subconscious plan of entrapment.

I have asked many men, "What were you thinking before you did this?"

They would not be able to tell me. They have not taken time to examine their thought processes enough to see what is happening.

4. *The hunt.* Next, the addict actually moves toward the object of his fantasies. For Jim the hunt began when he started his car and pulled out of the office parking lot. He knew he was going to get a magazine. It was only a question of which store and which magazine.

Nathan's hunt would begin when he dropped off his daughter and headed toward the red-light district. As soon as Bill ended one relationship, he would begin to hunt for the next one. In fact, wherever Bill was—restaurant, street corner or Bible study—he was hunting.

As the hunt progresses, neurotransmitters are released in the brain and adrenaline is released into the bloodstream. Dr. Gerald G. May says these nonsubstance addictions (stress, spending or sex addiction, for instance) are just as powerful as their chemical counterparts (drugs, alcohol and so on).[2] The closer the man gets to the right cable channel, magazine or woman on the corner, the more intense the intoxication becomes. Why does this cycle seem irresistible to the person caught in it? Because it is a perversion of a God-given process. The cycle was intended to awaken a husband and wife's desire for sex even at times when they are preoccupied by the demands of everyday living.

Married couples can testify to times when they have gone without intercourse for days or weeks only to find that a certain touch or look from the spouse kicks everything into high gear. When this power is awakened, their senses come alive and they move hungrily into each other's arms—even at two in the morning.

The purpose of this God-given mechanism is to strengthen the marriage bond. But this force becomes corrupted in the cycle of sexual addiction. Just as fire warms and comforts when restricted to a fireplace but destroys when it strays into the room, igniting carpet and draperies, sexual power too is intended to flow within clear boundaries. When it oversteps those boundaries, it becomes destructive.

5. *The connection.* This is the step where the addict dials the phone sex number and hears the operator's voice. Or opens the magazine and "connects" with the centerfold. Or is told by the woman at the bar that she will go home with him. The connection can be with a real person or

a symbol. Regardless of which it is, the addict experiences the illusion of acceptance. This emotional bonding makes him forget how lonely he is. At this point the sexual and emotional release is only moments away.

6. *The act.* The addictive cycle builds to its crescendo. Nothing matters now but orgasm. This is not the loving, passionate intercourse experienced by a healthy Christian couple. This is a release of the pent-up sexual energy that has masked the emotional pain underneath.

7. *Fulfillment.* At the moment of ejaculation the addict feels overwhelming pleasure (that is, if everything has gone according to his fantasy). He has reached the chemical payoff.

8. *The letdown.* The letdown immediately follows orgasm. Like Jim, the addict always forgets about this part. For Sam and Nicole, this feeling concluded almost every sexual act. Why? Because Nicole couldn't abandon herself to a man who did not allow her the freedom of sexual individuality. Sam sensed this halfheartedness and experienced it as rejection. Consequently, sex left them both wounded, not bonded.

The letdown is the lowest point of the cycle. It is here that the addict will do one of two things: get help or fall back into denial. For most, getting help is not an option, for two reasons.

☐ If he seeks help he will be required to stop. In spite of his misery and complaining, that is something he isn't ready to do.

☐ To seek help is to admit that something is wrong. The shame of that admission is more than his fragile ego can bear.

So until he reaches the end of his rope, he will continue falling back into denial.

9. *The vow.* And what form does this denial take? It takes the form of a vow. The addict will say to himself, "I won't tell anyone about this because it's not going to happen again!" At this moment he is utterly sincere. But in reality his ego is too fragile to admit that he is "wretched, pitiful, poor, blind and naked" (Rev 3:17).

He will offer a prayer of "repentance," make an apology, promise never do it again, and so on. But the problem is, he is still doing things *his* way. God requires that he bring other people into the struggle and submit to their counsel (Prov 11:14; 28:14; Jas 5:14). But he is unwilling to do this, so, from a biblical perspective, he has not repented at all. The vow, which *seems* to be a sign of genuine change, is actually an exercise in magical thinking. Real change is much more painful than buying God off with an apology.

One last thing about the vow. It is the only part of the cycle that is expendable. After years of broken promises (to himself and others), the addict will abandon vows entirely. Such a move can be good or bad, depending on the motive.

☐ If he discontinues making vows because they are deceptive, unbiblical and impossible to keep (see Mt 5:33-37; Jas 5:12), he is on the right track.

☐ But if he deserts them because he intends to act out again, his conscience is becoming desensitized.

One is a realization that he cannot change by his own power. The other is a resignation to the hardening of his heart.

10. The cycle resumes. The addict thinks his vow to be "serious with God" changes everything. In reality, his subconscious agenda is still the same. He still isn't open to the scrutiny of others; he hasn't acknowledged the true state of his heart; he continues clinging to his diseased thinking rather than to God's truth. It is only a matter of time before something triggers his unresolved pain and he feels the need to escape once more.

The letdown and the vow are not only the end of the cycle but the beginning of one to follow. The time between cycles may be hours or months (depending on the person), but the cycle will surely resume unless the addict recognizes his true condition. The cycle starts up again for another reason: the body has become conditioned through repetition.

Psychological Addiction?

Many think that sexual compulsion is only a "psychological" addiction: force of habit, weakness of character, or rebellion. Compulsion does involve these things, but the story does not end there. According to Dr. Jeffrey Satinover, repetitive sexual behavior alters the brain itself.[3] He says, "This ongoing process embeds the emerging patterns of our choices ever more firmly in actual tissue change."[4] Repetitive sexual behavior, practiced through the years, creates in the brain chemical releases upon which the addict becomes dependent.

When the sexual activity begins in early adolescence as a means of handling stress, loneliness or emotional pain, it is not long before a dependency is developed. This process can be well under way by the age of ten or twelve. Once puberty occurs, the young addict-to-be has the added dimension of orgasm to enhance the addictive experience.

According to Dr. Satinover, as the brain is forced to accommodate this constant release of opioids (opiumlike neurotransmitters), it creates neural pathways to facilitate their more rapid flow. The sexual addict becomes dependent upon the intense pleasure these chemicals create. The only experience more pleasurable is heroin use.[5]

An example of how this may work was demonstrated in research with laboratory rats. The rats were hooked up to electrodes that sent a current through their limbic system, stimulating the pleasure centers of the brain. The current was triggered each time they pressed a certain bar in their cages. Once they figured this out, they pressed the bar *thousands* of times per hour to the point of exhaustion![6] Clearly, they became addicted to the chemicals produced within their own bodies.

We are not rats, but our bodies function in similar ways. Incidentally, these pleasure centers in the brain are also stimulated by eating, drinking and exercise. Is it any wonder that millions of Americans are also using *these* activities in an addictive way?

Does this mean that sexually compulsive Christians are not responsible for their actions since a neurological addiction is at work? May it never be said! But it does explain why thousands of them find it so difficult to stop in spite of their Christian beliefs and repeated efforts.

This presents a good news/bad news scenario. The bad news is this: If you've engaged in compulsive fantasizing and behavior for years, you will struggle tooth and nail to stop—even if you love the Lord. The good news: if your brain was conditioned over time to respond this way, you can also *recondition it* if you are persistent. The biblical words for this are *sanctification* and *renewing of the mind.*

As the addict seeks to redirect his thoughts and choices, new neural pathways will be created to facilitate this change in direction. The systems in his brain will literally regroup into a new configuration as he redirects the thoughts and attitudes of his heart. This is good news, but it doesn't happen overnight.

Core Beliefs

The addict struggles at another level: the level of his beliefs about himself. The physiological changes we just discussed are a *result* of the addiction, not their cause. The core beliefs listed below—in concert with the sinful nature—are a *root* of the addiction.

The addict is being moved internally by a belief system he doesn't even know is there. If he hopes to be free of his sexual compulsion, he will have to understand this system. In *Out of the Shadows*, Dr. Patrick Carnes lists these beliefs as follows:

1. I am basically a bad, unworthy person.

2. If you really knew me you wouldn't love me.

3. I can't depend on others to meet my needs—I'll have to meet them myself.

4. Sex is my greatest need.[7]

Core belief #1. The idea of being a bad, unworthy person almost sounds Christian. It is not. Though Scripture talks about our sinfulness and unworthiness to inherit eternal life, that is not what this belief is referring to. This belief moves the sex addict toward a sorrow that approaches despair—just the opposite of the *healthy* shame (godly sorrow) that Paul describes in 2 Corinthians 7:10.

Though all of us have a certain degree of shame (thanks to original sin), the sex addict has a double portion. He has it as a result of his behavior (healthy shame) and as a result of being shamed as a child for things that were perfectly normal (toxic shame).

He was often belittled for expressing certain feelings, making mistakes or being too needy. When he wanted affection he may have been told, "Quit holding on to me like a clinging vine!" When he wanted attention, "What do you want now? Can't you see I'm reading my newspaper?" And when he didn't understand something, "What's wrong with you? Are you stupid?"

Christian families often convey similar messages (though with a "biblical" twist). For example, "Don't you know Jesus doesn't like it when you are sad/mad/bad?" or, "I know Daddy and Mommy aren't home very much, but we have so much to do at church" (translation: "The ministry is more important than you are").

In adulthood the shame-based person may be insecure and passive. Or he may project an aura of self-confidence to hide the fear that lurks below. But the real proof that he is operating out of core belief #1 is the fact that he abuses himself and perhaps others through sex. If his sense of self-worth were as biblical as he claimed, he wouldn't debase himself through sexually addictive behavior.

Core belief #2. The fear of exposure ("If you really knew me you wouldn't love me") is also something picked up in the family of origin. Painful interactions within the family taught the sex addict that it was not safe to be himself. The external niceness, achievement or rebellion only covers the raging loneliness within.

As an adult he has now perfected the double life: the man he presents to others versus the man he is when no one is looking. Not only does he expect rejection from others, he expects it from God. According to the addict's theology, God is too holy to step into the muck of his sinfulness and brokenness and lead him out. So he continues lying about this part of himself by not bringing it into the open.

Core belief #3. The sexually broken Christian believes that he himself is the only person who can take care of his needs. Some have argued with me when I suggested they might be operating from this base. They would tell me how much they loved the Lord, how much respect they had for Scripture and how much they loved people. Yet when I pointed to the way they actually lived, they had to admit that their faith might have been in these core beliefs rather than Christ. James says it well: our true beliefs are demonstrated not by our *claims* but by our *actions* (see Jas 2:14, 17-18).

Though the addict's relationship with God may be real enough, it does not go far enough. If you know someone who is not talking honestly about his sexual sins, lives as though he has it all together, and takes his unmet needs to compulsive sexual behavior, you are looking at someone who lives by core belief #3.

Core belief #4. This is the hardest one to admit. But if I seek something sexual every time I'm in need, it is obvious what my "god" is. Though we like to believe we are basically God-fearing people, the Scripture says, "There is no one righteous, not even one; there is no one who understands, *no one who seeks God*" (Rom 3:10-11).

We may seek him when the rent is due, when we need power for ministry or when our child is sick, but when the fragile base of our self-esteem is in danger, we tend to fall into addictive behavior, leaving God out of the picture.

If the Bible says anything about human nature, it says we are idolatrous. That doesn't automatically end when we are born again. As born-again Christians we now have *two* natures: one is bent toward God and one toward idolatry. Even when the new nature grows strong, the old idolatrous nature is still there—waiting to spring into action. That is why John warns, "Dear children, keep yourselves from idols" (1 Jn 5:21).

Our idolatry is expressed in ways unique to each of us. Some express it in obvious ways: occultism, homosexuality, sex addiction or substance abuse. Other idolatrous behavior is less obvious: finding worth through position, status, the approval of others, the accomplishments of one's children or achievements in ministry. Each of these things can be used to bypass going to God.

No one lets go of idolatrous attachments easily. This is especially true for the sexual addict. Remember Jim, the one who used pornography and masturbation? He was extremely challenged when I confronted him about this behavior.

"Jim, you say that Jesus is your Lord, yet every time the going gets tough, you turn to pornography."

"I know what you're saying is true. But—I'm going to be honest with you, Russell—I'm not sure I can do this."

"What do mean?"

"I mean, I've tried to pray and read the Bible when I was lonely. It didn't help."

"Is that what I'm telling you—'pray and read'?"

"Well, aren't you?"

"No. Mechanical Christianity won't help you. I'm talking about a relationship with God that invites him into the pain. But that can't happen if you use sex to *mask* the pain every time it comes to the top."

"What's God going to do for me when I'm hurting that bad?"

"Well, he's not going to wave a magic wand over you. Jim, you don't know it yet, but you are actually in a good place. Other Christians can go on with their lives without confronting their brokenness, but you don't have that luxury."

I continued, "Because of the pain you're in and what you've used to manage it, your life is starting to come unraveled. It's a good news/bad news proposition. The bad news is that because of what you're dealing with, you won't be able to play church as a lot of people do. If you do that, you won't make it. The good news is that if you let Jesus and a few others into this area of your heart, you will begin to heal and experience an intimacy with God that the average Christian knows nothing about."

Jim left my office that day feeling greatly encouraged. He has begun to reach out to a couple of men in his church whom he can trust. He has also begun turning to God in the face of his pain. It has been agonizing for him. Without the old addictive props to hold him up, he has hit bottom emotionally several times—the very thing he feared would happen if he didn't have porn to "save" him. But slowly he is realizing that God cares even when the loneliness threatens to engulf him.

Conclusion

Sex addiction is not only about moral weakness. It also involves chemical changes in the body that we cannot ignore. These changes have taken decades to occur and will require extremely hard work to undo. The addiction cycle is also a powerful force in its own right; it must be understood and worked through with the help of others. Likewise, as addicts we have a series of beliefs that support the addictive behavior. These beliefs must be exposed and refuted on a moment-by-moment basis if we hope to be free.

We have now laid the foundation for an understanding of sexual addiction. In the chapters ahead we will take an in-depth look at how to dismantle each of the components of this problem.

3

Where
We Start

Essential One:
Aligning Ourselves with God

Our sexual struggles are complex, so where do we start when it comes to solutions? We start by exploring (1) biblical recovery, (2) biblical sexuality and (3) biblical spirituality.

The church is in desperate need of recovery. A recent survey showed that when it comes to being faithful to our spouses, there is only a 2 percent difference between conservative Christian men and those who do not know the Lord.[1] Forty-one percent of men are also involved with X-rated movies, phone sex, pornography and nude clubs.[2]

Statistics like this show that we have adopted (or maybe never left) the mores of the world. If we hope to recover some type of sexual health, especially if we are compulsive, then we have to take seriously our first essential: *We must embrace Jesus Christ and the document that reveals his nature and directives—the Bible. Without this initial, basic step no genuine recovery is possible.*

1. Biblical Recovery
Two things about the recovery movement seem to trip up thoughtful

Christians. First, some in the movement have introduced concepts and practices that are foreign or outright hostile to biblical thought—ideas like determinism ("I have no responsibility for my actions—they are all a result of my dysfunctional family"), or the idea that happiness should be our ultimate goal.

Let us not make the mistake of throwing the baby out with the bath water because we hear some of these ideas—spurious as they may be— mingled with the gospel. We must also guard against the tendency to reject truth because it is spoken in psychological terminology rather than "Christianese." Psychological jargon is not automatically unbiblical.

For instance, some Christians reject the concept of "addiction" because they have heard it used in our culture to excuse sinful behavior. Though excusing my behavior is not a biblical thing to do, admitting I have an addiction is. Scripture teaches that a person can indulge in sinful behavior so often that it begins to control his mind, will and destiny.

Paul warns Christians not to indulge in behavior that characterizes unbelievers. If we do, we can perpetuate the same compulsive forces in our lives that enslave them:

So I tell you this, and insist on it in the Lord, that you must no longer live as the Gentiles do, in the futility of their thinking. They are darkened in their understanding and separated from the life of God because of the ignorance that is in them due to the hardening of their hearts. Having lost all sensitivity, they have given themselves over to sensuality so as to indulge in every kind of impurity, with a continual lust for more. (Eph 4:17-19)

This is a perfect description of the downward spiral of sex addiction. Paul says the problem begins with faulty core beliefs (futile thinking). These core beliefs begin to cloud our judgment and knock out our discernment (darkened understanding). This causes us to avoid closeness with God. We may go to church or even be pastors, but the flow of the Spirit is cut off to this needy area of our hearts (separated from the life of God).

This separation from the life-giving flow of God is a result of our false belief that we don't need God to touch this area, or that God cannot or will not touch it. Paul calls such beliefs "ignorance" and states that they flow from a heart that is growing increasingly hard.

The next thing the sexual addict experiences is a dulling of conscience and emotion (loses all sensitivity). In an effort to feel *something,* he will seek out greater emotional highs (give himself over to sensuality). The old sexual thrills become boring, and new, more risky fantasies and behaviors must be introduced (indulges in every kind of impurity). This causes the obsession to take over more and more of his life (continual lust for more).

The addiction comes to have a power of its own. Even if you are only what I call an internal sex addict, you will still find the desires inescapable without outside help. Proverbs 11:6 says, "the unfaithful are trapped by evil desires." The Lord Jesus goes even further and indicates that if we are sinners (and who isn't?), addiction is present somewhere in our lives, "I tell you the truth, everyone who sins is a slave to sin" (Jn 8:34).

> **ESSENTIAL ONE**
> We must embrace Jesus Christ and the document that reveals his nature and directives—the Bible. Without this initial, basic step no genuine recovery is possible.

Sin is the ultimate addiction, one to which none of us is immune. Therefore, it stands to reason that the addictive nature of sin would express itself in some of our lives in the unique form of sexual addiction.

Some Christians have a hard time with the label "sex addict." They feel it is a negative way of identifying oneself. Biblically speaking, the preferred label would be "child of God" (see 1 Jn 3:1-2). However, I also see the wisdom of naming the particular sin to which I am prone. The people in A.A. who say, "My name is George, I'm an alcoholic," are reminding themselves that they have a proclivity toward alcohol addiction and cannot afford to drop their guard.

If I engaged in sexually compulsive behavior for ten or twenty years before turning to Jesus, it is absurd for me to say, "Thank God that's all behind me now!" A lot of believers justify such thinking, based on a misinterpretation of 2 Corinthians 5:17: "If anyone is in Christ, he is a new creation; the old has gone, the new has come!"

As life-changing as the new birth is, we still have to ask the question, What *exactly* does the new birth change? We know that it alters our position before God and imparts all the benefits of Christ's death and resurrection to us instantaneously (see Rom 6:1-11; Eph 2:4-6; Col 1:13). It also gives us the potential to live a life that is pleasing to God. But here's where our thinking becomes simplistic and unbiblical. The new birth gives us the potential, but not the *guarantee,* of a holy life. Peter explains it well:

> Now that you have purified yourselves by obeying the truth so that you have sincere love for your brothers, love one another deeply, from the heart. For you have been born again, not of perishable seed, but of imperishable, through the living and enduring word of God. Therefore rid yourselves of all malice and all deceit, hypocrisy, envy, and slander of every kind. (1 Pet 1:22-23; 2:1)

Peter says there are two types of purity: the purity that God imparts to us freely at regeneration (salvation) and the purity that we ourselves develop *by obeying the truth* (sanctification). This second type of purity is not automatic; it is something we must continually strive for, based on the gracious power the new birth makes available. Peter acknowledges that the divine work in our hearts is eternal and enduring, but it is up to us to cooperate with this work and "rid ourselves" of the lifelong behaviors that preceded our conversion.

The idea that I can be nonchalant regarding my addictive sexuality because I am a "new creation" is the height of unbiblical naiveté. I may not want to wear the label "sex addict," but if addiction is there, I'd better wake up to its existence in my life.

The label "sex addict" is not a contradiction of my status as a child of God any more than is Paul's labeling of himself as "sinner" (see 1 Tim 1:15-16). James applied the same label to believers (see Jas 4:8), but, again, that in no way contradicted their position in Christ. In fact, owning the sexual addict within me is something that, if I work through it honestly, will actually move me closer to true holiness.

The Dysfunctional Church

If we are going to embrace Jesus Christ and his Word in our pursuit of wholeness, we will have to take an honest look at the church. The true church has always based its teaching on biblical truth. But the church also consists of fallible men and women who may *apply* that truth in a way that contradicts its intent.

A good example of this is the high degree of dysfunction among Christians. The astonishing thing is how this dysfunction is proclaimed as a biblical lifestyle. The three rules of any dysfunctional family are don't talk, don't feel and don't trust. Unfortunately, these rules are well established in the church.

Don't talk. When one believer shares with another that he is questioning his faith, doubting the reality of Scripture or wanting to have an affair—what kind of response is he likely to receive? Many times it sounds something like, "Oh, brother, you shouldn't talk that way! Just trust in God, and he will work all that out for you." Translation: "I don't want to hear it, and you are not allowed to voice those kinds of thoughts here."

Many of us have learned to say only what is acceptable to the Christians around us and not make waves (just as we learned these things in our families growing up). The problem of dishonesty within the church is not new. Paul understood it and exhorted us to resist it: "Therefore each of you must put off falsehood and speak truthfully to his neighbor, for we are all members of one body" (Eph 4:25).

Don't feel. This rule states that some emotions are acceptable and others are not. Again, this is the way lots of us were reared as children. We were permitted to feel happy, obedient or agreeable, but not afraid, angry or sad. Now, as adult Christians, we have carried that same thinking into the church.

Don't trust. When something is shared in private, and it makes its way back to us as a "prayer request," we conclude that we cannot trust other believers to keep a confidence. Or if we share something in a moment of vulnerability and are rebuked for feeling that way, we learn that we can't trust other Christians to hear our feelings and respond compassionately. This reinforces what many of us have believed since childhood: no one can be trusted.

I love the church with all my heart. That is why I am jealous for the church and angry when it fails. My affection for the body of Christ, however, cannot keep me from speaking out when I see the dysfunction of the world masquerading as spirituality in its ranks.

A Healing Environment
I long for the day when the church is truly a healing community where its

members are not expected to have it all together but are allowed to be what the Bible says they are—broken. This doesn't mean allowing people to continue unchecked in sinful lifestyles, but it does mean responding to them as Jesus does.

When he encountered those trapped in sinful lifestyles, he didn't bring the law down on their heads. He saw beyond their behavior to the underlying need. A good example is his treatment of the woman at the well (see Jn 4), to whom I referred in chapter one. She was a hardened, cynical person who had been used up in five failed marriages and was "playing house" with a new guy.

Jesus was compassionate and told her what she really needed to hear—without getting bogged down in some moral crusade. And it changed her life. To put it simply, he was kind to her. As Paul says, "God's kindness leads you toward repentance" (Rom 2:4).

The body of Christ must learn to remain both biblically solid and consistently compassionate. This is the only environment in which the sexual addict can experience healing. I believe this healing environment will prevail once average Christians understand the depth of their *own* sin and brokenness. When they do, they will have no trouble embracing the addict as he walks through his.

2. Biblical Sexuality

All we have to do is look at the divorce rate, society's open promiscuity, the illegitimate birth rate and the epidemic of sexually transmitted diseases (including AIDS), and we can see what happens when a people allow their feelings and glands to dictate their sexual behavior.

Those who are sexually addicted must figure out once and for all what the Bible teaches on these issues. This head knowledge will not save us, but we must at least have an intellectual basis for our sexuality, one that is founded on Scripture. If we will then *embrace* that knowledge and attempt to walk it out with the help of others, we will begin to see the profound wisdom behind what many consider "archaic" rules.

Pornography

Regardless of what the libertarians may say, pornography is destructive at a social level. In the 1970s many thought porn was harmless and, in fact, beneficial. In reality, the period of "openness" since then has seen the number of rapes double.[3] Pornography has come a long way from the "dirty pictures" of the sixties and seventies. Now it depicts women being raped, wives being battered and children being molested. A percentage of all pornography, even so-called "soft porn," promotes brutality toward women.[4]

The Attorney General's Commission on Pornography found that much of the porn industry is supported by organized crime. This "industry" rakes in billions of dollars a year (more than the record and film industries combined). If you are one who buys these magazines or videos, remember that you help supply these billion-dollar profits that are so helpful to crime syndicates throughout the world.

Unfortunately, these facts are usually not enough to motivate the sex addict to stop using porn. What motivates him is his inner emptiness. The satanic power of pornography goes beyond organized crime and the objectification of women. It presents a lure even more sinister than that: idol worship.

In pornography we fulfill the words of Paul: "They exchanged the glory of the immortal God for images made to look like mortal man and birds and animals and reptiles. . . . They exchanged the truth of God for a lie, and worshiped and served created things rather than the Creator—who is forever praised. Amen" (Rom 1:23, 25).

Ancient people had their images of men, women and animals. Modern people have the same images; we have just dispensed with everything below human life forms. No one can argue that in all of creation there may be nothing more striking than the female human body. But the glory of womankind was intended to point us to the glory of her Maker. When we stop short (as we do in pornography), we are worshiping the creature rather than the Creator.

A tradeoff has taken place. Those of us who use porn are taking our deep hunger for love to a sexualized goddess rather than to God himself. Though it is natural to want sex or to be charmed by a woman's body, the overwhelming compulsion of pornography should be a signal to us that this is about more than sex.

Christians who use pornography are attempting to satisfy legitimate needs for love, both human and divine—and satisfying neither kind! But the deception that perfect fulfillment is just one magazine or video away keeps us coming back.

Masturbation

Masturbation provides the payoff of pornography. It enables the addict to skip all of the demands that a mature relationship involves and relate to the fantasy woman in the magazine, video or computer. What about those who use masturbation without the aid of pornography? Does the Bible have anything to say about this? Let's address that question now, because the issue of masturbation is an important one for the sexual addict.

The reference that many use to condemn masturbation is the account of Onan (Gen 38:8-10). The context of this verse, however, indicates that God's reason for killing Onan was not his ejaculating on the ground but his refusing to impregnate his brother's widow in order to continue the family line. Out of spite, he withdrew during intercourse just before ejaculation. God saw his selfish, stubborn heart and judged him accordingly. It wasn't a case of masturbation.

Another reference that is cited is Leviticus 15:16-18. It says that when a man has an ejaculation, his body, any soiled clothing and his spouse must be washed and considered unclean until evening. Do these verses prove that masturbation is an "unclean" act? Not at all. Masturbation is not even mentioned. The text implies that the ejaculation occurred during either sexual intercourse or a nocturnal emission ("wet dream").

God's concern here was of a sanitary nature, not a moral one; it isn't immoral to have sex with your wife. The people of that time had inadequate health codes, which resulted in the routine spread of disease and infection. That is the reason the Israelites had regulations regarding discharges and other bodily functions (see also Lev 15:8, 19-31; Deut 23:12-14).

When it comes to the subject of masturbation, we can find no clear biblical prohibition, but, as we shall see, it definitely violates biblical principles. We can recognize at least four reasons why a sexually addicted person should avoid masturbation:

It usually involves fantasizing. Though Scripture may not specifically forbid masturbation, it definitely forbids lust. Matthew 5:28 exhorts a man not to fantasize about having sex with anyone who isn't his wife. If we are honest, we will have to admit that when we masturbate we usually see (and, in many cases, require) a mental picture of some woman in a sexual setting. Masturbation and fantasy almost always go together.

It is a mismanagement of emotions. When the sexual addict is bored, lonely or angry, he masturbates. This is no different from what the alcoholic does when he experiences some type of stress, except that the alcoholic chooses a six-pack rather than an orgasm. Instead of working through the emotions and understanding what they mean, the sex addict short-circuits the whole process by masturbating. When we do so, we are kept perpetually stuck in adolescence rather than learning to process our feelings in a mature, adult manner.

It keeps the door to our addiction open. We may justify masturbation by saying, "At least I'm not fornicating or running around on my wife!" There is some truth to this, but when we engage in masturbation, we are probably thinking about old behaviors and experiences or dreaming up new ones. This practice waters and fertilizes the roots of sexual addiction in our minds. That is a perfect setup for a fall.

It violates biblical sexuality. From Genesis to Revelation, whenever sexuality is discussed in a positive light, it always refers to the basic truth of two people, a man and a woman, being joined together. It was meant to be a *shared* experience. The idea of "solo sex" doesn't fit into this picture at all. The only alternative to monogamy, as far as Scripture is concerned, is celibacy (see Mt 19:4-6,10-12), not masturbation.

The single person must learn, as challenging as it is, to redirect his sexual energy into worship and service (more about that later). The married sexual addict has a similar task. He must learn to channel his sexual energy toward his wife and toward the Lord.

Adultery

A man commits adultery because of his false belief that *this* person can give him unconditional love. He may be very intelligent, like an adulterous seminary professor I counseled, but he has a total lack of discernment. A man who commits adultery proves his underlying ignorance of God's ability to meet his need. That is why Proverbs 6:32 says, "A man who commits adultery lacks judgment; whoever does so destroys himself."

The adulterer has no idea how much this "love" is going to cost him. He will find, if he stays in the relationship long enough, that the other woman has some of the same problems his wife has. Consequently, he ends up having to deal with the very things he was trying to escape.

Add to this another destroyed marriage and a couple of shattered children, and we can see why Solomon says: "For a prostitute is a deep pit and a wayward wife is a narrow well. Like a bandit she lies in wait, and multiplies the unfaithful among men" (Prov 23:27-28).

One man I counseled had spent his money on prostitutes and was discovered by his wife. He pleaded with her not to leave him, but she was too wounded. She took his two sons and left the state. Because of alimony and child support he was stripped financially bare. He lost his family, his car and his home. He was sleeping in a friend's office by the time it was all over.

> Do not lust in your heart after her beauty
>   or let her captivate you with her eyes,
>   for the prostitute reduces you to a loaf of bread,
>   and the adulteress preys upon your very life. (Prov 6:25-26)

Finally, some think that since they haven't lost everything, God's warnings must not apply to them. They have secretly had other women, yet their marriages haven't fallen apart, and God still uses them in ministry. Keep in mind, however, that God used Samson in spite of his sexually addictive behavior (Judg 16:1-3), but his sin eventually caught up with him and he died in disgrace. The price of adultery simply isn't worth it. As legitimate as the unmet need may be, the arms of another woman is no place to get that need met.

3. Biblical Spirituality

The sexual addict can have a good support system in his life and be growing in his grasp and application of biblical sexuality, but if he fails to walk in biblical spirituality, the other pillars will eventually topple as well. To the degree he is broken, to that degree he must connect with the Lord and with the Lord's people if he hopes to recover.

The Church

If the addict is not plugged into a vital body of believers, he had better get that way fast. Scripture is very clear about our need to meet together as Christians: "Let us not give up meeting together, as some are in the habit of doing, but let us encourage one another—and all the more as you see the Day approaching" (Heb 10:25).

We can all find reasons not to be involved in the church: It is full of hypocrites, we don't like the style of worship, the pastor goes on too long, it has too many cliques, everybody is shallow, they're always asking for money—and so on. (Did I miss any?) But the author of Hebrews implies that if we follow the example of others and bail out of the church, we may not make it.

We die without encouragement. We simply aren't strong enough to make it on our own without the help of others. As crucial as a support group may be in the life of a sexual addict, it cannot replace the family of God. We need to be in a place where we worship with other believers. We need to hear what the Spirit is saying to his people through Scripture and through divinely appointed leaders. And we need to nourish authentic relationships with those in the body of Christ who may not struggle with sexually addictive behavior.

What we cannot afford, however, is simply to show up on Sunday morning and think that will supply all we need. We have to seek out those within the body of Christ who want to have real fellowship. Peter said, "Above all, love each other deeply" (1 Pet 4:8). To love deeply will require that we work through the disagreements and misunderstandings that are bound to come up within a Christian community and push ourselves beyond superficial relationships.

Along with this, the recovering sex addict will have to guard against two things: premature ministry and the refusal of others to let him grow at his own pace. According to Scripture, God often took decades to work in an individual's life and strengthen him as a person before he pressed him into service.

But God's way is not our way. We continue pushing people into ministry who are not ready for it, and then we scratch our heads when they crash and burn. The addict will have to pursue relationships within the church but avoid the temptation to enter into service prematurely.

When the addict is not walking in a vital relationship with the Lord, his ministry becomes a means of gaining approval and significance, to artificially bolster his self-esteem. The discerning pastor or elder will be able to recognize this need and encourage the wounded believer to experience healing before jumping into a flurry of activity.

I understand that we often grow while we serve others. But if a sexual addict also has a compulsive attitude toward work (and many do), he must be lovingly discouraged from getting busy in the church until he has been allowed to rest, receive and grow. Further, if he lacks the discipline simply to worship and connect with others, he won't be any good for ministry.

Prayer

God will not bless a prayerless recovery. No support group, book, tape, church service or revival meeting can carry us if we are not interacting privately with God through prayer.

Engaging in real prayer is one of the most difficult things in the world to do, not because it requires specialized skills, but because it requires us *to be relational*. And that is the very thing the sex addict is not.

We may have used relationships to get sex or acceptance, but that is not the same as being relational. Those who use impersonal substitutes like porn and masturbation have an even harder time. The good news is that we can learn. If we are serious about getting to know God, we can confess our superficiality and self-centeredness and beg him for assistance. If we will do so, we will already have begun relating to him honestly.

We must also learn to use our God-given powers of imagination to see the glory of Jesus Christ as revealed in Scripture. We need to envision his resplendent beauty. We need to see the compassion and mercy on his face. In doing this, we connect with the One our heart *actually* craves, rather than turning to a counterfeit with a pretty face and an hourglass figure.

Finally, when it comes to prayer we must avoid the extremes of emotionalism and legalism. We will have to guard against the tendency of using God like another drug (emotionalism) or manipulating God through a formula of phrases and practices (legalism).

God is a person to be related to, not a principle to be mastered. We will learn that God always fulfills his Word, but not always in the manner or timing we want. Eventually we will come to appreciate God's uniqueness instead of being frustrated by it.

Scripture

"Well, I know I *should* read the Bible. . .", he said as he shifted nervously on the couch. *I wish I had a dollar for every time a counselee has said this to me,* I thought. I often hear this guilty statement when I explain that Bible study is absolutely essential to recovery. Whenever we approach the church, the Bible or prayer with a "should," we've already moved toward legalism.

Imagine a man who has just fallen off the deck of a ship. It is the dark of night. The water is so cold his body begins to numb. Several sharks move in and begin swimming a circle around him, and he sees the ship pulling away. He is screaming for help at the top of his lungs and fearing the worst when suddenly he sees a tiny form on the back of the ship throwing something—it is a life preserver.

Can you imagine this man saying to himself, "Well, I know I *should* grab this thing but . . ."?

The Word of God is the only hope we have if we want to understand God, ourselves and healing. If we avoid the study of Scripture or do it with a feeling of obligation, we are as senseless as the man questioning whether he needs the life preserver. Yet many sexually broken people fail to study their Bibles seriously. Here are some of the reasons why this happens:

I'm too busy. But we find time to eat, watch TV, go to the game or act out sexually. In other words, we all have time for what is important to us. Anyone can set aside twenty or thirty minutes to read, if he wants to. Many of us just haven't incorporated Bible study into our day the way we have made time for other things.

It's too hard to understand. This is the only excuse that has a grain of truth to it. The Bible is not an easy book. It was written by people of another culture who had their own unique history, poetry, idiom and method of storytelling.

Not only that, the theological truths of Scripture would be hard to grasp
no matter in what language, culture or era they were communicated. As
intimidating as it may sound, I believe it is well worth the trouble.

With patience and persistence anybody can have a working knowledge
of Scripture (Mt 11:25). We may have to read every section several times
and prayerfully ask for illumination. However, if we continue over the
years to chip away at it, the essential truths of Scripture will begin to rise
to the surface, and the once difficult book will become more and more
clear.

I find it boring. I see two reasons for this. First, we don't understand it
(as stated above). Second, it's hard for Scripture to compete with the
excitement of MTV, James Bond, and a thousand other visual and auditory
distractions bouncing around in our heads. Becoming quiet enough to hear
what the Bible is saying is a difficult task, but it is one we can learn.

It isn't relevant to me. A careful reading of Scripture shows that the men
and women described in its pages experienced the same things we do—
bills, marriage problems, unruly children and sexual impulses. They were
weak, sinful, doubting and inconsistent, yet God worked in their lives. We
can learn much from them.

The stories are too fantastic. In our so-called scientific age, many of us
balk at believing that biblical miracles are actual events. If we feel that
what we are reading is a fable, it will be hard to take it seriously. A person
can always do a little research into the archeological, scientific and
philosophical validity of the Bible. Plenty of good authors have answered
the objections that are raised against Scripture.

Another remedy is to take a chance and obey God in some of the things
he says. If you do this, you will find yourself in situations where he has to
intervene in miraculous ways. After experiencing minor miracles of your
own, you won't have a problem believing that God can also do the major
ones described in Scripture.

I can live without it. This is one statement few of us would openly admit
to. But the fact that many of us don't study Scripture proves this is our core
belief. For those who don't want to rationalize Scripture out of their lives,
let me offer some simple guidance. Any books, commentaries or study
helps that assist you in delving into the Word will certainly be beneficial

(the *Recovery Bible* has been a big help to many), but I also recommend
that you simply read the Bible and let its naked truth speak for itself. A
helpful tool for doing this is the memory device A, E, I, O, U:[5]

A. Ask questions. In your reading ask yourself questions like these: "To
whom is the writer speaking? What is the context? The historical significance? The personal significance?"

E. Emphasize words. Take a verse and emphasize each word in order to
get the full meaning.

I. In context. Find out if the verse is general or has conditions. Is it for
all time or a certain time?

O. Other Scripture. Find relevant passages in other books of the Bible
that help explain the one you're looking at. Remember, the Bible is its own
best interpreter.

U. Use it. All the Bible study in the world won't help if you don't apply
what you learn.

Conclusion

To recover from sex addiction we have to embrace this first essential:
intimacy with Jesus Christ and cooperation with his Word. This will be
fleshed out as we pursue a recovery that is consistent with biblical
revelation.

We must wrestle with the truths of biblical sexuality (rather than
mouthing evangelical clichés). We must return to the basic disciplines of
the Christian life: fellowship, Bible study and prayer. We will have to work
hard to keep these from becoming dead forms. True growth will not take
us beyond these things; it will take us deeper into them.

4

Enlisting
the Help
of Others

Essential Two:
The Power of
Genuine Friendship

Nathan stood nervously in front of the audience. He had agreed to give his testimony at our promotional dessert, but I could tell he was scared. I could also tell he was determined. "I wouldn't be here today," he began, "if it wasn't for people who loved me." I couldn't help feeling proud of the changes that had taken place in his life.

It seemed like only yesterday that Nathan was sitting in my office saying he couldn't stop soliciting prostitutes. Until then he had tried a do-it-your-self recovery complete with prayer and Bible study, but nothing had changed. Those disciplines hadn't helped him, because he left out a crucial element: other people. But now look at him! Once he was terrified of anyone's ever knowing his secret. Now he was telling a crowd of four hundred people how Jesus had saved him from sexual addiction.

I snapped back to the present in time to hear him say, "I tried everything, folks, but nothing worked until I involved people. *It's people that make the difference!*" Nathan was right. No lasting change in addictive behavior will come without the help of others. This brings us to our second essential: *We must establish at least one to three supportive relationships for the purpose of accountability. Without this we will be deluded regarding our motives and unable to control our behavior.*

When a sex addict is told he must share his secret with others, he feels one thing—terror! But there is something he may not have considered: keeping it a secret also keeps him in bondage. Scripture says that without the regular involvement of another brother, we *will* fall into self-deception and sin: "See to it, brothers, that none of you has a sinful, unbelieving heart that turns away from the living God. But encourage one another daily as long as it is called Today, so that none of you may be hardened by sin's deceitfulness (Heb 3:12-13).

This is one of those clear statements that many of us ignore. We may go to church on Sunday morning and Wednesday night. We may even attend a men's meeting. But few of us allow our lives to come under the regular scrutiny of others. That is why we don't change.

Jim was not pleased when I shared this with him. He said, "Are you telling me that I won't stop using pornography and masturbation unless I spill my guts to other people?"

"That's exactly what I'm saying."

"I don't feel comfortable with that. Why can't *God* just work in my life?"

I asked Jim if he had gotten saved, joined the church and grown as a Christian all on his own, or if God had used others in the process. He admitted that others were instrumental along the way.

"If God used other people to accomplish every major thing he's done in your life, what makes you think *this* will be any different?"

"I think I see what you're saying."

Jim realized it was his fear of exposure that kept him from involving others, not his supposed dependency on God. Unfortunately, as long as he kept his behavior a secret, no one could stand in its way. This type of transparency is essential if we want to experience four things: accountability, support, understanding of our motives and continued growth and healing. Let's look at each of these.

Accountability

Every sex addict has a ritual. It may be like Jim's: going to certain stores to buy magazines and then masturbating in a particular room of the house. It may be like Nathan's: feeling the need to escape certain emotions and driving to a certain part of town to pick up prostitutes.

There are as many rituals as there are people. Maybe you've tried to stop yours, but failed. Either it starts up again or you discard it only to pick up another. As Dr. Satinover says, this ritualized pattern has become deeply embedded in the neural network of your brain and will not be overcome without the help of others.[1] You will have to find a counselor, pastor or trusted friend to whom you can divulge your ritual. That person will need to know the specifics of your ritual: where, when, what, how and with whom. He will need to know what you've done in the past and what you are doing now. And you will need to ask him to confront you and find out how you are doing at any given time.

If certain parts of town, certain activities or certain experiences are a stumblingblock for you, you must be accountable to this friend on a weekly or daily basis *about that very thing*. Anything less will spell defeat.

You must exercise accountability regarding nonsexual issues as well. If you tend to be passive and avoid doing things you should do (for example, taking the initiative to spend time with your wife and kids), you need to confess the specifics and give this friend permission to ask about it. If you have struggles with certain emotions, beliefs or attitudes that set you up for failure, you have to bring someone else into that struggle. Determine not to live in isolation anymore but to live an examined life. One last thing: accountability is not only about reporting failures but learning to reach out *before* you fail. So it should also include sharing your positive progress and successes. Each step forward may seem small to you, but report it with joy and gratitude.

Support

Accountability and support are not the same thing. True accountability requires that someone have the grit to make you uncomfortable if that is needed. Support requires that someone have a love that will stand by you even if you are sinning repeatedly. It's great when you can have both in one person. But not every helper is at that level, which is one more reason to have at least two or three.

You may have noticed that I keep saying you need *men*. Can't a woman provide this type of support as well? Certainly. But a different dynamic is at work when we seek this kind of help from members of the opposite sex. Though God used a female therapist to open the doors of healing in my own life (this was especially important since I had so many "mother issues"), other men have had the greatest impact.

Relating with other men provides a healing opportunity that doesn't include the potential risk of sexual attraction and interaction—unless, of course, you struggle with homosexuality, in which case there is still a need for healthy same-sex relating.[2] A supportive relationship is about more than stopping sexually addictive behavior. It is about addressing the underlying need for love that the addictive behavior represents.

Have you ever wondered why David said of Jonathan, "Your love for me was wonderful, more wonderful than that of women" (2 Sam 1:26)? David had all the women he could want. But his relationship with Jonathan was unique, partly because sexuality did not enter the picture. This freed both men to love each other in a way that met deep needs in both of their hearts.

I realize that this level of relationship is threatening to most men, but the need is there. No one understands a man like another man. Yes, women have a unique place in our lives, but they can't call out our masculinity in the way another male can. They can "mother" us and contribute to a sense of security (in a good marriage relationship), but they lack the ability to speak to a man's façades with a man's language.

Though men do not do this naturally (and we are socialized not to), I suggest it is God's will. What did Peter mean when he said, "Above all, love each other deeply" (1 Pet 4:8)? Was he talking only about opposite-sex relationships? If he was talking about men loving men, surely it was intended to go beyond Super Bowl parties and prayer breakfasts.

I have had the privilege of knowing at least two men on this level. One is my friend Nick. The other is my friend Brian. I've known Nick for fifteen years. God first knit our hearts together at a men's retreat. As our relationship grew, we felt greater and greater freedom to share the grisly details of our lives with each other.

Nick confided in me about his sexual addiction before I even knew what sexual addiction was. We spent hours praying, talking and learning how to feel. At first our wives thought we were obsessed with each other. But after a while they realized that the love we shared as friends indirectly made us better husbands. Nick lives three hundred miles away now, and I see him only once or twice a year. But when we are together, we pick up right where we left off.

Brian is a gift from God to me. After years of meeting at Denny's at six in the morning, we have come to know each other on a level I can describe only as intimate. Brian knows everything about me that my wife knows. And I know him to that same degree.

We have spent hundreds of hours together, sharing biblical truths and humiliating revelations. Not only can I share my sins with him, but I can share something else with him that only God and my wife are privy to—my dreams. Instead of reacting with envy or insecurity, he rejoices with me and encourages me to believe the impossible.

> **ESSENTIAL TWO**
> We must establish at least one to three supportive relationships for the purpose of accountability. Without this we will be deluded regarding our motives and unable to control our behavior.

Brian and I don't have stars in our eyes—we know each other's dark sides all too well. But because we have boasted to each other about our weaknesses, the power of Christ has come to rest on our friendship (see 2 Cor 12:9-10). These relationships with Brian and Nick have taught me that I can experience genuine affection and trust in a man's world.

Understanding Our Motives

Years ago I was talking with a friend who was trying to convince me that everyone misunderstood him. He said, "They just don't know my heart. But *I* know my heart!" I was speechless. I couldn't believe that someone with his biblical understanding could make such a statement when Scripture clearly says, "The heart is deceitful above all things, and desperately wicked: who can know it?" (Jer 17:9 KJV).

The fact is we *don't* know the depravity and self-deception our hearts are capable of. We all have blind spots. To believe otherwise is stupidity at its finest. That is why God's Word tells us repeatedly that we must be open to the correction of others (Ps 141:5; Prov 12:15). No one needs this outside input more than the sexual addict. We need others to be instruments of God to point out our addictive logic. The core beliefs addressed earlier are a good example of this addictive logic. Here are some other examples:

"I know our affair was wrong, but God revealed his love to me through that woman!"

"If my wife would lose some weight and be a little warmer under the covers, I wouldn't need to do this."

"It's not pornography; it's the beauty of God's creation!"

"Hey, every guy needs an outlet."

"God understands."

"If I don't get it every day or so, I have physical pain."

"I have more sexual needs than the average man."

Every one of these justifications (and others I could cite) have been used by Christians I've worked with. When I, or someone else, attempted to point out their flawed reasoning, they often responded sorrowfully, "You don't understand."

Ah, but I do. I have used some of the same rationalizations in the past, and the scary thing is I believed them too! We think the Bible is talking only to *other* people when it says, "There is a way that seems right to a man, but in the end it leads to death" (Prov 14:12).

The sexual addict desperately needs others to reflect back to him what they see him doing. That is why Scripture says, "In the multitude of counselors there is safety" (Prov 11:14 KJV). One of the most effective places for this to happen is in a confidential group setting. In time and with the right leadership, a group of men can learn things about themselves that they would never discover in isolation.

Not only can the members of the group confront sexual behavior and addictive logic, they can also help us see the sinful and self-protective ways we relate to others. These self-protective relating styles are just one more way we keep ourselves from having to trust or risk.

Being passive, trying to fix everybody else and using anger to keep others at bay are things many of us have been doing since childhood. For us it is a normal part of our personality. Unfortunately, it keeps us from facing some hard truths and experiencing healing. All of this comes out in a group setting.

Obviously, this level of self-discovery can be frightening. I believe that is why our sinful nature instinctively avoids it. But you must fight this tendency if you are a sexual addict, because only as you disclose your feelings to others will you truly come to know yourself. I believe this painful self-disclosure is a part of what our Lord meant when he talked about losing our life so we could find it.

Continued Growth/Healing

Jesus died for two reasons: first, to reconcile us to God (Rom 5:10; 2 Cor 5:18-20; Col 1:22) and second, to reconcile us to each other (Mt 5:23-24; Col 3:12-13; 1 Jn 3:11, 16; 4:10-12). It's no accident that recovery from sex addiction (or any addiction, for that matter) requires the involvement of others. As long as we say, "I'll take care of this myself," we commit two errors: We persist in the erroneous idea that we don't need other people, and we frustrate the very thing for which the Son of God died.

He came that we might have life, and that life is experienced in fullness by means of an intimate fellowship with other believers (see Ps 133; Jn 10:10). The addict, as a result of his addiction, lives in alienation from the body of Christ. He may be involved in some relationships and ministry, but no one knows him *as he really is*. And without this level of self-disclosure he will never heal or mature in the truest sense.

Our tendency is to look for change through the amassing of knowledge. We go to seminars, conferences and retreats, hoping that God will miraculously take us to the next level of spiritual growth. But we err if we think that growth and healing come merely through the accumulation of data. Growth and healing always have and always will come through relationships with God, self and others.

Many of us have read enough Christian books on recovery to start our own second-hand bookstore, but we still fight fiercely with addictions and compulsions. Why? Because we talk with a great deal of "recovery savvy," but we often omit the hard work that recovery requires. Proverbs 14:23 says, "All hard work brings a profit, but mere talk leads only to poverty." The need is not necessarily for more information but for the application of it.

This is where intimate, soul-searching relationships come into play. We don't learn merely by reading and hearing; we learn by watching. It is as you open your soul to others (which is always scary if you're really doing it) that you get close to them. And as you get close to them, you will see what they are doing right. The apostles delighted in teaching this way and invited others to get close enough to observe their lives (see 1 Cor 11:1; Phil 3:17; Jas 2:18).

No technique, prayer method, principle or book (not even this one) will do the trick. A relational wound requires a relational solution. That is why we have to get down to the dirty business of knowing each other as we are.

Whom Can You Really Trust?

You may be saying, "Well, it all sounds good, but I don't know anybody that I can *trust* with that kind of information." You have a valid concern. Many in the church can't keep a confidence; many are unaware of the deeper issues and reluctant to hang in there for the long haul. "Many a man claims to have unfailing love, but a faithful man who can find?" (Prov 20:6).

As challenging as it may be to find "a faithful man," you must prayerfully do so. If there is no one in your church that fits that description, look elsewhere. If there is no one in your area, consult the resources in the back of this book. But, whatever you do, find someone who can keep your feet to the fire!

Probably God has already placed someone like that in your life. It may be a counselor, pastor, elder or friend. If you think you know someone who is a good candidate, you are going to have to step out. This kind of relationship must be entered into gradually and mutually. Here are some guidelines:

☐ Look for someone who demonstrates mercy and compassion.

☐ He must also have a grasp of truth and not be afraid to confront.

☐ He must be able to hear the details of your story without backing away in disgust or fear.

☐ He must be a person who is comfortable with the expression of emotions and not require that you conceal yours.

☐ He should be someone who doesn't have to fix everything with a Bible verse or Christian cliché.

☐ He must be able to share with you how *he* is broken as well (if he doesn't think he is, he can't help *you*).

☐ He must not repeat what you share without your permission.

☐ He must know that you are likely to lie to him.

☐ He must be regular and specific in the questions he asks you.

☐ He should be someone who can rejoice with you over little victories.

☐ He must love you and not see you as a project.

Obviously, we don't share the intimate details of our lives with *everyone*, but we must do so with a few. Our Lord modeled this for us in his relationship with Peter, James and John. Though he didn't need them for accountability, he did look to them for friendship and support (see Mt 26:37-38). If *he* needed companionship with other men, don't you?

Many gather once a week in men's groups to study a book or discuss theology without ever taking the risk of really knowing each other. But if you are not sharing your life and feelings with other men in a way that sometimes scares you to death, you are not being transparent. Isolation is bad for any man, but for the sexual addict it is fatal.

Conclusion

Change is not accomplished through education alone. God uses intimate relationships to do his greatest work of change. It is through these relationships that we learn to report to another about our feelings and choices. They provide some of the love and acceptance that we mistakenly look for in sex. And this honest setting enables us to see our true motives, giving us power to choose a different course. Finally, it is in relationship to other growing men that the holes in our development start to get patched. If this book moves you toward honest relationships, it has accomplished its purpose; if not, it is a waste of good paper.

5

Understanding the Mold

Essential Three:
Exploring Family Issues

Mat and Cindy were an attractive couple. They were missionaries to Africa who had come back to the United States to get counseling. Mat had struggled with pornography for years, but his wife was very understanding. In fact, she was too understanding. As I began asking questions about Mat's growing up years, Cindy jumped right in and spoke for him. "Oh, if you're going to ask about his parents, I wouldn't bother."

"Why's that?" I inquired.

"Because Mat takes full responsibility for his actions. He doesn't *believe* in blaming his parents."

"Is that true, Mat?"

"Absolutely. Whatever mistakes my parents may have made has no bearing on what I'm struggling with now."

I commended Mat for not making his parents a scapegoat as so many do. But I also sensed that I wasn't getting the whole story. I asked him if he could humor me while I asked him some questions about his family anyway. He agreed. As I began probing into his relationship with each parent, I found that he was uneasy about discussing his father. So I pressed on the nerve a little more.

"Mat, I notice that you are reluctant to discuss your relationship with your dad."

"I'm not reluctant. It's just that my father was a good man, and I see no point in bringing him into this. We weren't as close as we could have been, but I have a lot of respect for him."

"Based on what you've told me, it does sound as if he was a good man. But when you said that you weren't as close as you wanted to be, I noticed that your eyes started filling up with tears."

Mat looked at me for a moment and then turned away. I could see his face contorting as though he were in pain. He began heaving huge sobs and buried his face in his hands. Cindy was noticeably uncomfortable. After regaining his composure, he sat there shaking his head and staring at the floor. I allowed the silence to ring in our ears for a few minutes. Then I spoke up.

"You're feeling a lot of pain, aren't you, Mat?" He nodded his head.

"Could it be that your relationship with your dad has affected you more than you realize?" Another nod.

"I'm going to suggest, Mat, that your hunger to be loved by your dad has more to do with your sexual addiction than you think. And one of the reasons you haven't overcome the addiction is that you haven't taken an honest look at that relationship."

I have witnessed many such scenes. Experiences like these and the way Scripture explains them have caused me to see the importance of our third essential: *We must courageously and honestly explore the dynamics of our original family. Otherwise, formative trauma will be hidden to us, and false self-concepts will remain intact.*

Though some blame everything on their parents, I have also seen the opposite extreme. Well-meaning Christians may say, "Forget the past, you are a new creation! It's time to grow up and stop blaming everyone else for your life." As "spiritual" as this sounds, it is unbiblical and counterproductive.

Where the Ache Originates

Nathan (the man who struggled with prostitution) came from a severely abusive background. His alcoholic father would literally throw him against the wall for such "major" infractions as interrupting him in conversation. Nathan never got close to his dad because he was too busy walking on eggshells around him and trying to stay on his good side.

Because there was no real bonding between them, Nathan also felt cut off from his own masculinity. As a teenager he did all the things he thought would "make him a man": football, girls and drinking. In a few years he, like his dad, had developed alcoholism. Eventually he entered Alcoholics Anonymous.

Getting sober was a significant accomplishment for Nathan. Unfortunately, he traded one addiction for another and began frequenting prostitutes. After becoming a Christian he stopped—for a while. But that behavior came back, because he didn't know any other way to quiet the ache in his soul. He was using women to affirm the masculinity that his father had failed to nurture.

Luke struggled with voyeurism and pornography. He would spend endless hours looking through windows or searching for magazines by the roadside. After six months of marriage, his new wife had had enough and demanded that he get help. Not only was Luke a Christian, but he had been reared by parents who were missionaries. They were not alcoholics and child abusers, like Nathan's parents; they were decent and respectable people.

Luke got along okay with his father. It was his mother from whom he felt detached. She was a kind woman but somewhat cold. She herself had been brought up by parents who demonstrated almost no physical affection. As a young boy Luke would wrap himself around her leg and ask for kisses, but she was uncomfortable with his "hanging" on her all the time. This made him believe something was wrong with him for wanting to be close.

One day when Luke was about nine years old, he came home early from school. As he walked through the living room, he caught sight of his mother sunbathing on the back porch. And like many of the women in that part of Mexico, she did her sunbathing in the nude. Luke immediately averted his eyes. But when he realized his mother hadn't seen him, he crept behind a chair and stared at her glistening body. His heart was pounding, and he had an erection. His mind swam with terror and euphoria. When his mother sat up, he quickly recovered and ran to his room.

Luke felt guilty but strangely warmed at the same time. He couldn't get the image out of his mind. In the months that followed he found himself wanting to see her again. He even sneaked into her bedroom and made tiny cuts in some of her blouses, hoping she would inadvertently expose herself when she wore them.

Though it is not uncommon for a boy to be struck by the accidental sighting of his mother's body, Luke was affected very deeply. When he saw her on the porch that day, he felt a hunger for the infantile nurture he never had. The combination of his "mother hunger" and the nudity that seemed to satisfy it became a snare. The seeds of sexual addiction had been sown.

Obviously, choice was involved for both Nathan and Luke. Even as children they were accountable for the things they did and the sins they committed. But here is an important point: They were *not* responsible for the vacuum in their hearts created by unmet developmental needs. This hunger for parental love set them up to meet their need in sinful ways. Proverbs 27:7 says, "To the hungry even what is bitter tastes sweet."

Why Dig Up the Past?

What can you do now about what is past? Obviously, you can't go back in time and have all of your nurturing needs magically fulfilled. But if you don't take an honest look at how those deficits were created in the past, you are doomed to continue seeking false solutions in the present.

Exodus 20:12 says, "Honor your father and your mother." Does this mean that you are supposed to lie about ways in which they may have sinned? Not according to the prophet Ezekiel. He was told, "Will you judge them? Will you judge them, son of man? Then confront them with the detestable practices of their fathers and say to them: 'This is what the Sovereign Lord says'" (Ezek 20:4-5).

Scripture goes on to say, "Do not be like your fathers and brothers, who were unfaithful to the LORD. . . . Do not be stiff-necked, as your fathers were" (2 Chron 30:7-8). And Stephen said to the elders of Israel (who "honored" their fathers *and* their way of doing things), "You stiff-necked people, with uncircumcised hearts and ears! You are just like your fathers: You always resist the Holy Spirit!" (Acts 7:51). Obviously, honoring our parents does not mean following in their sins or pretending they didn't hurt us.

All parents make mistakes. The ways they wound their children may be mild or severe. But to believe that your parents were perfect is a denial of original sin. If you believe the Bible, you must believe that you live in a fallen world. That fallenness has affected everything from the ecosystem to the interaction of your family. Not only that, but if you refuse to take an honest look at the way your parents may have hurt you, you will hurt your children in the same ways. This is how family dysfunction (or fallenness) is transmitted from one generation to the next.

Let Us Search

Jeremiah said, "Let us search and try our ways, and turn again to the LORD" (Lam 3:40 KJV). Contrary to what many in the Christian community assert, taking a look at ourselves and our past is not a matter of "navel gazing" but of obedience to God. Paul said, "A man ought to examine himself" (1 Cor 11:28). And David said: "When you are on your beds, search your hearts and be silent" (Ps 4:4).

> ESSENTIAL THREE
> We must courageously and honestly explore the dynamics of our original family. Otherwise, formative trauma will be hidden to us, and false self-concepts will remain intact.

When Scripture tells us to search, examine and consider our way of doing things, we obviously have to look at our behavior and that of our families. So much of what we do, think and feel is influenced by our upbringing. We cannot effectively stop sinning if we are blind (or resistant) to considering the mold from which we sprang.

Some things in the present will *not* change unless we deal with the past. Let me give an example from David's life. During his reign a famine hit Israel and lasted for three years. When David asked the Lord what was going on, God said, "It is on account of Saul and his blood-stained house;

it is because he put the Gibeonites to death" (2 Sam 21:1).

The Gibeonites were a Canaanite tribe that was promised special protection by Joshua (Josh 9:15-20). Later, King Saul attempted to wipe them out in clear violation of Joshua's oath (2 Sam 21:2). This series of events in the past was what God wanted David to deal with in the present. It would have been a mockery for David to say, "No, Lord, I'm not going to worry about the past. That's all behind me now. I'll just look to the future and trust in you!"

Areas of Brokenness
We've established that our upbringing has more influence on us than many of us are willing to admit, and many of us know that deep-seated issues remain in our hearts. But how did our family help create these, especially if our family seemed like a fairly good one? To answer that, we will take a look at three areas: (1) shame, (2) emotions and (3) beliefs.

1. Shame
The issue of shame is one of the most misunderstood and overlooked aspects of Christian growth. I have yet to meet a sexual addict who doesn't struggle with it. Yet many fail to discern the presence of shame in their lives and the consequences that follow it. Let's look at three basic kinds of shame: consequential shame, fallen shame and abandoning shame.

Consequential shame. The first type is felt by the sex addict every time he acts out. It is the natural consequence of sinning against himself and God. It is the voice of conscience raised in protest (if he hasn't deadened it completely). We can be thankful that when we start getting our sexual behaviors under control, this type of shame begins to diminish.

Fallen shame. Fallen shame is a good thing if properly understood. This is the shame we inherited from our original parents in the Garden of Eden. Though we are forgiven by the blood of Jesus, we still sense how far we are from God's perfect holiness. This shame need not make us run and hide as they did, for we can have assurance, through God's grace, that we are safe in his presence from being judged (see Rom 5:1; 8:1-2; 1 Jn 3:19-20).

Fallen shame will be with us, to some degree, until the Lord returns, because if we're honest with ourselves, we will always be aware of our humanness and imperfection. But it need not make us feel condemned. Paul looked forward eagerly to the day when believers in Jesus will be completely free of fallen shame (see Rom 7:24-25; 8:22-23).

Abandoning shame. Abandoning shame is the experience, whether conscious or not, of feeling worthless—at a core level—because of how others have treated us. This type of shame is the hardest to heal, especially since many of us don't even know it is there. This shame is created by experiences of physical, sexual or emotional abuse in childhood.

As a child you were completely dependent upon adult caregivers to interpret reality to you. If that interpretation was skewed (example: "You are good for nothing!") then you assumed—because you were a child— that the adult must be right. This kind of verbal and emotional abuse makes us feel worthless. No wonder Scripture says: "The tongue has the power of life and death" (Prov 18:21).

Where abuse is a sin of commission, neglect is a sin of omission. Emotional neglect can be just as devastating in the long run but harder to pinpoint. That is why Paul clearly commands, "And, ye fathers, provoke not your children to wrath: but bring them up in the nurture and admonition of the Lord" (Eph 6:4 KJV). Many parents provide a home, education and other opportunities for their children but fail to give them nurture. They simply don't know how to speak and act in ways that impart life to the core of their child's being. This leaves the child internally impoverished, even if he lives in a nice home and goes to the best schools.

The only way for parents to prevent this, especially if the parents weren't nurtured in their own childhoods, is to be in a deep, nurturing relationship with God, receiving the nurture that he is able to supply to his children. You can't give what you don't have. If God is not telling *you* on a regular basis, "You are my treasure—I love you and find incredible value in you" (see Is 43:4), you are unlikely to be saying it to your children.

This is the kind of affirmation and nurture parents were intended to give (see figure 1).

To the degree that they do not give it, they are not performing their God-given function. Thus, they are "dys"-functional, and the child is left with a corresponding deficit. This deficit is what the child often seeks to fill, in adulthood, with something sexual (see figure 2).

Emotions

The sexual addict is also impaired when it comes to emotions. The two extremes I've seen (and have experienced in my own life) are fanatical feelings and frozen feelings.

Fanatical feelings. This person says, "See, I'm very healthy and in touch with my feelings. I can cry, be angry and be passionate." Every woman to whom he is attracted starts as "the most wonderful girl in the world" only to become "the girlfriend from hell" a short time later. He is intense about evangelism, worship and sex. He is equally intense in his negativism when things don't go his way.

Frozen feelings. The person with frozen feelings is cut off from his emotional self. Those closest to him assume he doesn't have any feelings. He does; he just doesn't show them in obvious ways. He believes his flat disposition is normal, even spiritual. Nonetheless, he cannot escape his need to feel something. So he reserves the experience of passion for sex, binge eating or the adrenalin of workaholism.

Where did these two learn to express emotions? The fanatical-feelings person is sometimes reared by parents who are outgoing and expressive. But usually he comes from a family that is "dead" emotionally. His exaggerated emotions and behavior are a means of overcoming the sterile environment in which he grew up.

The frozen-feelings person is just the opposite. He is usually carrying on the family tradition of "stability." In his family, expression of strong emotion was discouraged by example and implicit teaching. When he was sad, he was told, "Nobody likes a person who pouts." When he expressed joy, he was told to "settle down." He learned at an early age that acceptance was based on suppressing his unwelcome emotions and expressing only family-authorized feelings.

Unless the addict takes an objective look at his family of origin, he will assume that his family's way of expressing emotion was the "right"

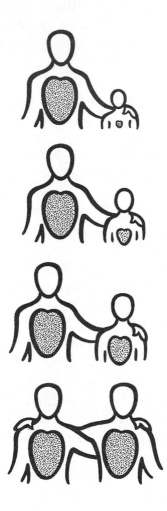

Figure 1. Healthy parental nurturing bond. In a healthy parent/child relationship, the adult (whose sense of self is symbolized by a solid core) is able to reach out to the child (whose sense of self is only partially formed) with loving words, attitudes and actions. Though God is the only one who can *complete* this process (during and after adolescence), the parental bond has a profound impact on the child's healthy sense of self as the child grows toward maturity.

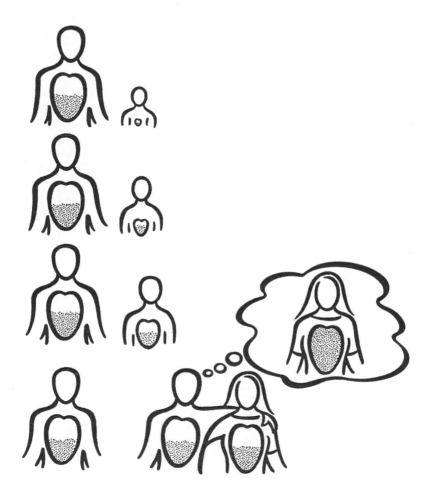

Figure 2. Inadequate parental nurturing bond. In the formative years, the sex addict has an inadequate or nonexistent nurturing bond with the parent(s). This is symbolized here by the lack of touch between the two. Consequently, the child develops no healthy sense of self (though he may have an exaggerated, unhealthy sense of self by which he compensates). In early adolescence and adulthood he will reach out to one or more females who he perceives will provide the fullness he lacks.

way. Or he may rebel against their patterns and end up living in the opposite emotional extreme from them. Either way, he forfeits his God-given personality and becomes vulnerable to sexual addiction in every area where he expresses (or fails to express) his emotions in a biblically healthy way (see table 1).

Unhealthy emotional life	Healthy emotional life
It's not okay to feel sadness or depression. If I do, something must be wrong with me.	My family may have shamed me for feeling these emotions, but they are a natural part of living in an imperfect world (Ps 31:9-10; 38:1-9; Lam 3:3-9; Mk 14:32-34; 2 Cor 1:8-9).
If I allow feelings of sadness to surface, they will engulf me.	Scripture commands me to mourn and tells me there is a blessing for those who do, not for those who suppress grief (Mt 5:4; Rom 12:15).
A real Christian overcomes grief quickly, because "the joy of the Lord is my strength."	My family may not have given me permission to grieve, but God understands that some pain takes a long time to work through (Eccles 7:3-4; Is 53:3; Rom 9:1-2).
If I show anger, people will know how unspiritual I am.	It is possible to demonstrate passionate anger without falling into sin (Mk 3:5; Jn 2:14-17; Eph 4:26).
I can be angry only at injustices done to others (e.g., abortion, child abuse), but not at those done to me.	I can allow myself to feel anger at *personal* injustice and express it in appropriate ways (Gen 31:36-42; Acts 16:36-37).
If I am still angry about something, it proves I haven't forgiven.	If I am still angry, it may mean that I have extended *superficial* forgiveness without following the biblical command to confront first, then forgive (Mt 18:15-17; Lk 17:3).
If I don't get along with everyone, it shows that I am not a loving Christian.	As a healthy man, I know I will not get along easily with every person in my life (Lk 6:26; Rom 12:18; Gal 1:10).

Unhealthy emotional life	Healthy emotional life
If I really loved God, I would want to pray, read the Bible and serve all the time.	I do not assume that I am supposed to be perfect, as my parents may have expected; I work through my imperfections patiently (Phil 3:3, 12).
Taking care of my own needs is selfish. I'm supposed to take care of others first.	I know how to take care of my body, soul and spirit so that I have something to offer someone else (Mt 11:28; Mk 4:38; 6:31; Lk 2:48-49).
If I were really Spirit-filled, I wouldn't have such strong desires for sex, security, revenge and so on.	Some of my sinful longings are misunderstood legitimate needs. But even after working through those, the sinful nature will still be present—no matter how godly I am (Rom 7:15, 19, 21; Jas 3:2; 1 Jn 1:8).
Exploring how my parents reared me is just an attempt to put the blame on them.	I am honest, like David, about any abandonment issues I may have (Ps 27:10). I look for truth even if that brings me into conflict with my parents (Mt 10:34-37).
Feeling hurt or resentful about childhood experiences proves that I am still immature.	As a child I may not have had the luxury of expressing hurt or anger. As an adult I now have that freedom (Eccles 3:1, 4).
Focusing on my feelings is selfish. Obedience to God is what matters.	I know how to feel, consider, express, journal about, or seek counsel regarding my feelings (Prov 20:5; Ps 139:23-24). Peter denied Christ because he had not taken time to acknowledge and deal with his weaknesses (Mt 26:33-35). I don't want to make the same mistake.

Table 1. Contrasts between healthy and unhealthy emotional life

Beliefs

We've talked about different sets of beliefs, but we need to examine what we believe about the family itself. If we've been brought up in a dysfunctional setting, as many of us have, we were taught to look at that family in certain ways.

These unhealthy attitudes are the result of being reared in an atmosphere where open discussion of problems was not permitted. Many of us realized that if we wanted to be accepted, we were going to have to "go along." Unfortunately, many of us went along with unhealthy or sinful ways of relating. They became normal to us.

Some of us find it extremely difficult to see our families with true objectivity. It is helpful (for some, mandatory) to work through the problem with an objective third party such as a counselor, therapist or pastor. Even this is a challenge, however, because of a deep sense of being "disloyal" by daring to question the dynamics of our families.

Not only is the sex addict himself prevented from growing and healing because of his fear of family disloyalty, but his children are harmed as well. Since he does not permit himself to be angry about any abusive or neglectful treatment he received at the hands of *his* parents, he is unable to be angry when he does the same things to his own children.

In this instance, anger is necessary in order for him to change. But if anger was not a "family-authorized emotion," he will tend to suppress it. In fact, if he is a Christian, he will tend to see anger as "unspiritual." This is a good example of family beliefs being superimposed upon Christianity.

Conclusion

If you want to experience healing from sexual addiction, you will have to take an honest look at the profound influence your family has had on you. You will have to examine the beliefs, perceptions, emotional responses and warped self-image you may have inherited. You must not allow family loyalty to stand between you and loyalty to Jesus Christ. Exploring the past is indeed a biblical means of understanding the present and moving into the future.

6

The Myth
of No-Fault
Victimization

Essential Four:
*Taking Ownership
of Our Choices*

I hit the stop button on the cassette recorder. As I lay on the bed and stared at the ceiling, I mulled over what I had just done. At the suggestion of my therapist I had taken time to chronicle my life from as far back as I could remember to the present.

I had recounted my parent's divorce, our move to Texas, my mother's days in the honky-tonk lifestyle and all the pain that followed. As I looked at the pile of cassettes on the bed, I realized I had recorded twelve hours' worth.

As a result of going through my personal history, I had learned two things. First, the pain in my heart was even deeper than I thought. My lack of bonding with my mother, coupled with her example of sexual promiscuity, contributed to the formation of my own sexual addiction. This was becoming increasingly clear to me. The second thing I learned actually came as a surprise. God said to me as I neared the completion of my audio journaling, *Son, it wasn't your mother's abandonment of you that caused your sex addiction. It was your response to that abandonment that caused the addiction.*

My mind was reeling. Was God saying that my childhood pain had no bearing? Not at all. He was quick to empathize with my heartache. But what I understood for the first time in my life was that my mother's emotional abuse and neglect of me were not the origin of my present struggle—my own *choices* were.

True, I didn't have much information to go on as a seven-year-old. But it was the way I handled my brokenness—even then—that began charting my course. This truth has shown me the importance of our fourth essential: *We must understand how we responded to formative trauma and how that response is perpetuated today. Otherwise, we will remain stuck in self-defeating attitudes and behaviors, all the while blaming them on someone else.*

This is not a contradiction of the previous chapter. Our past pain and its effect are very real. But that is only one side of the coin. If we focus exclusively on that, we will never experience healing. The other side of the coin is our personal reaction to that pain. We may not have had the maturity to make better choices then, but we do now.

Before we take a look at making healthy choices, we will need to understand what choices we made as children. Those choices, along with environmental factors, helped shape our personalities, attitudes, world-views and sexuality.

When I Was a Child

Paul said, "When I was a child, I talked like a child, I thought like a child, I reasoned like a child. When I became a man, I put childish ways behind me" (1 Cor 13:11). Paul is saying that he abandoned his childish ways of doing things. The sexual addict has *not* abandoned this way of living. In fact, he has continued in it so long that he thinks it is the way adults act!

We are still trapped, as Paul said, in childish ways of communication, thought, reasoning and behavior. These childish coping mechanisms form the basis of our personalities and responses to life. They also make it possible for sexual addiction to continue unchecked. Let's take a look at these "childish ways."

Communication

Children are inherently self-centered. This is normal for them. But adults are supposed to have progressed beyond that. Unfortunately, the sex addict has not. Though he may demonstrate maturity in some areas, at the core of his being, where it matters most, he is still clinging to childish fantasies and behaviors. This is clearly evident in the way the sex addict communicates. I have seen several styles of communication among Christians who struggle in this area. I will call them the talker, the avoider and the blamer.

The talker. John was the traveling evangelist we met in chapter one. He was articulate and intelligent and didn't mind demonstrating it. He would make comments in the group about theology, church history and other impressive insights. These "insights" didn't help him stop having affairs, however. John was a talker.

I didn't say anything to John at first. I sensed that his fragile ego couldn't take it. But after he had been in the group for a while and had found out that we really did love him, I broached the subject.

"John, you have a lot of good things to share, and I know some of your comments have helped men in the group. But I'm wondering if maybe you don't hide behind your many words." I asked the others if they felt the same thing. They all nodded in agreement.

John responded, "You know, I think you may be right. I don't mean to do it, but I can see how I might be using that to cover my insecurities."

We commended him for his willingness to hear us and asked if he would like us to hold him accountable. He said he would. In the months that followed, whenever John would begin to wax eloquent, one of us would say, "Get to the point, John." He knew what that meant, and he would tell us what he was really feeling, instead of philosophizing about it.

The talker is like the child who tries to throw people off his trail by overwhelming them with information.

"Junior, did you steal this comic book?"

"No, Dad. I had a deal with Billy that if I helped him clean his room and also won our bet on the Rams game, he'd buy it for me! The guy at the store only *thought* he saw me take it, because I was just holding it for Billy. And . . ."

You get the picture.

The avoider. The avoider uses one of the most powerful weapons there is: silence. Don't get me wrong; the avoider can have his congenial side, but when the conversation gets too personal, he simply shuts down.

When he is cornered about his behavior, motives or whereabouts, he produces a hurt look and silently walks out of the room. He learned in childhood that this tactic is an effective way of keeping people out.

At first people take responsibility for causing the avoider so much "pain." But eventually they become enraged as they realize they are unable to penetrate his evasive wall of silence.

The avoider takes great pride in being a quiet man. He sees it as a biblical virtue. In reality, it is the way he unconsciously dodges his need for change. A truly adult approach would be to take ownership of his flaws and stop stonewalling those who invite him to step out of his comfort zone.

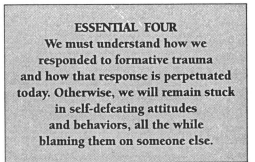

ESSENTIAL FOUR
We must understand how we responded to formative trauma and how that response is perpetuated today. Otherwise, we will remain stuck in self-defeating attitudes and behaviors, all the while blaming them on someone else.

The blamer. The blamer avoids taking personal responsibility by attacking those who catch him in a lie or sexual indiscretion. He immediately accuses them of being critical, suspicious or self-righteous. Since there is usually some truth to his accusations, he effectively silences most of his critics.

Mark Twain once said, "A man is never truly a failure until he blames others for his mistakes." The blamer's crying need is for courage to hear what others, including God, are saying to him. Because he holds to the first core belief of the sex addict ("I am basically a bad, worthless person"), he cannot endure any constructive criticism that seems, to him, to confirm his sense of worthlessness.

He has an extremely hard time separating what he does from who he is. Once he can see that he still has great worth to God and others *in spite of his real faults,* he will be able to hear what those faults are and begin correcting them.

Thoughts

"I thought like a child." Many of us can't use the past tense as Paul did, because we are still stuck in childish beliefs, perceptions and notions that protect us from having to take responsibility for our choices. In another place Paul calls these *strongholds* (see 2 Cor 10:4-5).

Fortunately, he says that these strongholds can be demolished and that we can experience transformation, if we will only change our thinking (see Rom 12:2). What are some of these patterns of thinking that keep us stuck? The main ones I've seen are egocentrism, centrism, animism and hopelessness.

Egocentrism. Egocentrism is normal for a child between the ages of two and six. Children at that age believe that they are the center of the universe and that they control everything around them.

The adult sex addict is still trapped in this egocentric worldview. If his wife politely turns down his sexual advances, he just knows it is because she hates him. It couldn't possibly have anything to do with her being tired, having a headache or needing some space. He perceives that many woman are either sizing him up as a potential sex partner or rejecting him on sight.

The addict's family, friends and employer are amazed at the way he makes everything be about *him*. But he really believes it is. He is frozen in that developmental stage of childhood that seeks the approval, notice and admiration of those around him. What he doesn't realize is that there *is* someone who wishes to give him that absolute, undivided attention he never received—Jesus.

Centrism. Centrism is that stage of childhood development where children are getting in touch with their inner world. A boy may spend hours in his room shooting at imaginary bad guys or drawing pictures of aliens and narrating to himself every blast from their phasers. He is in his own little world. This is a normal stepping-stone on his way to maturity.

The sex addict's fantasy life becomes more inviting and his investment in the real world diminishes. He may be content to sit with magazines or in front of X-rated movies for hours, tuning out his personal problems as he did in childhood.

This is the one place where no one ever rejects him, demeans him, refuses his sexual advances or stands against his unstoppable power. In his mind he is the undisputed master of the universe. He still carries a deep sense of worthlessness, but he compensates for it through his detailed fantasies of sexuality and aggression.

Instead of channeling his imaginative powers into productive things like problem solving, serious Bible study or intimacy with God, he squanders those powers on fantasies of perfect love, sex or power. He is still capable of harnessing his powers of concentration for positive ends, but he will lose more and more of this ability as the addiction progresses. When he has opportunity, he tunes everything out and goes to that place where he is free from the responsibility to grow.

Animism. Why do young children need dolls, teddy bears and action figures? Because they endow these inanimate objects with human qualities, giving themselves a sense of power and control. But as they mature, they are able to take more and more risks on their own instead of living vicariously through Barbie or G.I. Joe.

Many a sex addict grew up in a home where it was unsafe to take risks. He was not allowed to express certain feelings or entertain certain points of view that contradicted his parents. In that setting it was easier to find his identity through an idealized extension of himself: an object, super hero or celebrity. As natural as this is in certain stages of childhood development, we are intended to outgrow it.

For the addict, Superman has been replaced by Miss September or the "babe" in the front office. The young boy looks to comic book heroes with rippling muscles to affirm his masculinity. The adult sex addict looks to sexualized images of femininity to affirm that he is acceptable and desirable.

In its extreme forms animism doesn't even need a person. A piece of clothing may serve as a human representation or an object that can be used in a sexual way. This object becomes a fetish to which the addict can attach mentally, thereby avoiding the risk of real relationships. Pornography serves the same purpose.

Hopelessness. Hopelessness is not only a response to traumatic losses; it can also become a habit-forming coping mechanism. Children may lapse into this hopelessness because they don't have all of the information. My daughter once cried uncontrollably because her balloon popped. To her, all was lost. Because of her sobs she was unable to hear me telling her I would get another one out of the bag. It wasn't until it was blown up and placed in her clenched fist that she opened her eyes and chose to hope again.

For many of us a popped balloon was the least of our worries in childhood. Some of us had childhood years that were filled with parental abuse, rejection or just plain indifference. In order to keep our sanity, many of us had to let go of the dream of ever having our needs met in these relationships.

God graciously allowed us to find some semblance of security in achievement, outside friendships or a fantasy world of our own making. These were necessary to us in childhood. But when we become adults, the Lord challenges us to shed our juvenile coping mechanisms and dare to hope in something realistic.

The sex addict has given up hope to varying degrees. He may have given up hope that he will ever have a satisfying marriage, so he looks in vain to other women or pornography to fill the void. Others have given up on marriage altogether. They pursue the fleeting and—in the age of AIDS— dangerous search for momentary fulfillment in the singles scene. Others live in a lonely world of cable TV or computer porn.

Two things can be said about the sexually broken. First, their hopes for love and protection were often shattered in childhood. And, second, *they refuse to hope now* even though the Son of God is pleading with them. They cling to the familiar feeling of abandonment and rarely venture outside into the open spaces of God's love and grace. Why? Because they don't really believe it exists, or, if it exists, they believe they are not eligible for it. This is a repudiation of what they claim to believe.

In their opinion, their hopeless and cynical view of life justifies their acting out. But the voice of Jesus calls out to them, "I may not meet your needs in the ways you think I should or in the timing you desire, but I *will* meet your needs, if you lay down the hopelessness by which you shield yourself from pain."

Reasoning
"*I reasoned like a child.*" Not only does the sex addict persist in childish

thinking, but this thinking forms his intellectual base. This is a scary thought: What he perceives as deductive reasoning is actually circular reasoning, guaranteed to confirm his preconceived views. His mind works in a closed system that he *thinks* is open-mindedness. The only way to escape these cognitive distortions is to let someone with more wisdom point them out. But he can't do that, because if someone points out a flaw in his thinking, that will only confirm to him that he is stupid and therefore worthless. See why this trap is so hard to escape?

Leonard was a successful businessman and church elder who had hidden his porn addiction for twenty years. His wife didn't suspect a thing until one evening a police officer pulled into the driveway with Leonard in the back seat. Leonard had been caught masturbating in public. Sally's world came crashing down, and the two of them ended up in my office.

Over the next two years they both made progress in our groups. But something about Leonard always concerned me. Whenever someone would say, "Leonard, I think such and such is a problem in your life," he would stiffen and become defensive. What he was *hearing* was, "Leonard, you are a failure as a person! It does no good for you to even try!" At such times I would gently point out to him that the grid he was looking through was rusted. Several in the group pleaded with him to hear not only what they were saying but the love behind it. He insisted that everyone, including me, was "out to get him."

The situation escalated over the next six months. Finally I met with him and Sally in private in an attempt to reassure him of my love and concern. During our time together his wife turned to him and—with all the tact she could muster—mentioned something she was troubled about. Leonard heard it as a scathing accusation. When I pointed out to him what had just happened and how he had completely misinterpreted what she said, he sprang to his feet.

"Russell, you've never given me any credit for the changes I've made! Now you and my wife are *both* trying to shoot me down. Well, I'm not going to take it anymore! I'm out of here and I don't plan to ever come back!" With that he walked out of my office and slammed the door behind him.

Leonard was convinced that the whole world was out to get him. He wasn't even open to another possibility. In Leonard's childhood his alcoholic father *was* out to get him. But he began projecting his father's attitude onto everyone in an attempt to protect himself. This "reasoning" continued into adulthood with disastrous effects. His wife continues to grow toward emotional health and healing, but Leonard has left his recovery process and his thirty-year marriage, claiming he's been betrayed.

Childish Ways

What are some of these childish ways of behavior that persist in the lives of sex addicts? Though the answer to that could easily fill another book, I want to pinpoint two very important ones: dishonesty and passivity.

Dishonesty. Not only does the sexual addict lie to cover his addiction, he practices a more pervasive type of dishonesty as well. He is rarely honest about what he feels, unless he is very angry. When he is angry, he will say things that come as a complete shock to those around him. He will later come back and say, "I'm sorry. I didn't mean that, I was only mad."

In reality, he *did* mean it. What prevents him from saying it 90 percent of the time is his fear of rejection. He probably grew up in a family that prized "niceness" over honesty. In that setting the expression of genuine feelings is always punished in one way or another. Children must be taught how to express fear, anger and disappointment in appropriate ways. But most addicts were brought up in homes where anger was either the reigning tyrant or the "elephant in the living room" that no one talked about.

An addict with that background has an artesian well of anger inside, but he has never allowed himself to express it in appropriate ways. If he were a *real* Christian it wouldn't be there in the first place, right? You see how faulty messages from our families contaminate our theology.

The fact is that real Christians do get angry. And not just "righteously indignant" either. Men and women of God have struggled with anger for centuries. Their anger was often the result of mistreatment at the hands of others (see Ps 3:1, 7; 17:10-13; 35:4-8; 54:1-5; Acts 16:35-37; 2 Tim 4:14). Every bit of this anger was legitimate. Yet, if we heard someone in our church talk the way David or Paul did in the preceding verses, we would probably say, "Brother, you have to forgive. You know God doesn't want you to be angry."

In reality, God knows we will be angry, and he can handle it. We are the ones who can't handle it. We are afraid it will make people leave us. So we wear a nice "Christian" face and give people the impression that we never get mad. But every bit of it is a lie. It's no coincidence that Paul encourages us to stop lying to each other and to begin by being honest about our anger (see Eph 4:25-26). When you begin expressing your anger in appropriate ways, without concealing it, you will find that your need to act out sexually begins to diminish.

Passivity. Passivity is one of the worst problems sex addicts have to face. It prevents them from changing their thoughts, changing their behavior, obeying God or taking risks. Passivity is the feeling that could be expressed thus: "Oh, well, I can't do anything about it. Nothing ever changes anyway." It is one of the root sins that give rise to sexual addiction.

This too is a carryover from childhood. Addicts' repeated attempts to please their parents and win their affection were often futile. In response many develop a passive orientation to life. As adults they win the approval of others by niceness, but even that doesn't always work. In those cases they withdraw into the self-protective shell of passivity, where no one can hurt them.

Passivity has always had dire consequences in the lives of men. The very first man to demonstrate it was Adam. Instead of taking a stand, he "went along" and placidly ate the fruit (Gen 3:6). Abraham did the same thing. Instead of drawing the line and telling his wife "No. We cannot do this," he submitted to Sarah's agenda and fathered a child out of wedlock (Gen 16:1-2).

Eli is another example. He spoke to his sons, Hophni and Phinehas, about their immoral lives, but he didn't actively restrain them. God judged him severely for his passive response (1 Sam 3:13) and for seeking his sons' approval over the approval of God (1 Sam 2:29).

David, as outstanding as he was, gave in to his passivity and refused to take action when one of his sons raped his half-sister (2 Sam 13:1-21). After Absalom took matters into his own hands and killed his sister's rapist, David still refused to deal with the situation or work through the issues with Absalom (2 Sam 14:23-24). Only under duress would he even speak to his son (2 Sam 14:28-33). David's unresponsiveness so exasperated

Absalom that he eventually rebelled against his father and started a civil war that resulted in the deaths of twenty thousand men (1 Sam 15:1—18:7).

These examples from Scripture show that obvious immorality is not the only thing that can bring destruction to our lives. Passivity can be just as damning. The pacifist takes false comfort in the fact that he is not involved in "overt sin," never realizing that passivity is a form of rebellion.

Many sex addicts are real go-getters in business, ministry or sports. But in key areas of their lives, passivity has taken over. You had no control over the fact that your father was abusive, necessitating that you "disappear" into a passive shell in order to survive. Or you had no control over the fact that your father was Mr. Passivity himself and left you that legacy. Or you had no control over the fact that there was no father at all—no one to call out your true masculine initiative. But you are not a child now.

God wants to make you into a new man. A man who can be gentle and compassionate but who can stand up to danger and face it even when his heart is in his throat. Your desperate need is for courage—courage to face your fear of rejection and courage to face your fear of failure.

God makes that courage available to you, but you must step out and take hold of it. Let him show you what a man really looks like. Learn from the ultimate man, Jesus Christ. As you follow in his steps, you will find yourself facing your fears and running less often into the false security of sexual compulsion.

Conclusion

Face whatever pain may have been in your childhood and grieve it well. But don't blame your current state on childhood trauma. Place the blame where it belongs: on your response to that trauma, a response that in many ways you continue choosing today. Determine to abandon your childish ways of communicating, thinking, reasoning and acting. Declare war on "niceness" and choose to live according to truth, as your Master did. And, finally, see passivity as the cancer it is. Do these things, and one day you will be able to say like Paul, "When I became a man, I put childish ways behind me."

7

The Divine Caricature

Essential Five:
*"Will the Real God
Please Stand Up?"*

Jim was doing well and starting to develop genuine relationships with other men. His days of fantasizing at work and then going home to masturbate (as we read in chapter two) were practically a thing of the past. He was growing rapidly and feeling greatly encouraged—until today.

He had had an argument with his roommate the night before and had felt rejected. After his roommate left, he started feeling depressed and hopeless. He prayed, but nothing seemed to work. Even God didn't seem to care. He picked up the phone and dialed the number of his accountability partner. He wasn't home either.

With seemingly nowhere else to turn, Jim gave in. His four months of sexual sobriety came to a disappointing end. As he sat in my office, he shook his head in disgust and confusion.

"I don't understand, Russell. I was doing so well. I've been praying, reading the Word and reaching out to others. But after my roommate said those things, I just felt hopeless. I'm not making excuses, but why did I crumble like that?"

After finding out that his feeling of hopelessness was actually a feeling of worthlessness, I sensed there was a deeper issue we needed to look at. I grabbed a tablet out of my drawer and drew a line down the center of the page. At the top of the left-hand column I wrote "Dad," and at the top of the right-hand column, "God." I turned to Jim and asked him to describe his father.

"You know what he was like. We've talked about it before."

"Yes, I remember. But tell me again; how did the two of you get along?"

"Well, I felt like I could never please him, his standards were so high."

I wrote "perfectionistic" on the left. "What else, Jim?"

"He was distant. I know he loved me, but he had a hard time showing it."

I wrote "distant."

"Most of all I felt like a disappointment to him."

I wrote "disappointed." I could tell that Jim was wondering where I was going with this.

"Now, describe God to me. I don't want your Sunday-school answers but what you really feel he is like."

He proceeded to give me the Sunday-school answers anyway. When I pointed out to him that those weren't his beliefs the night before, he got more honest with me. He then told me he felt that God was disappointed in him. God was distant and too holy to relate to a sexual deviant like him. After writing his answers in the right-hand column, I turned the tablet around and showed it to him.

"What do you see?" I asked him.

"I see that the lists are almost identical."

"What does that tell you, Jim?"

The light went on.

I have learned that our behavior says a great deal about how we see God. We *say* that he is loving, kind and forgiving. But when the chips are down, we have a hard time believing it. At times like that we often fall back on some sinful behavior to comfort ourselves. Sexual addiction does not change in a lasting way until we face this issue. Our fifth essential is this: *We must explore the origins and content of our perceptions of God. Faulty thinking and responses must be corrected if we hope to develop trust and experience reparenting.*

We say we are Bible-believing Christians, but our behavior exposes a completely different set of beliefs. These beliefs about God are based not on the clear teachings of his Word but on our own previous experiences in other relationships.

A Hard Man

In the twenty-fifth chapter of Matthew we read a parable about three servants. Each was given a sum of money to invest for his master. The first two invested wisely and were able to double their allotment. But the third servant did nothing with his share. He buried it instead. His rationale for doing this is very interesting: "'Master,' he said. 'I knew that you are a hard man, harvesting where you have not sown and gathering where you have not scattered seed. So I was afraid and went out and hid your talent in the ground. See, here is what belongs to you'" (Mt 25:24-25).

The servant "knew" that his master was hard. Where did he get this knowledge? Certainly he didn't get it from observing the master. The master (who represents God) was just and equitable. The other two knew this. This servant, however, had a completely different view. The only way he could have developed this perspective was to observe others who were hard and then project that onto the master.

Where Did We Get This?

Like the servant in the parable, we tend to see God in a negative light. This is proven by our disobedience and fear. We don't believe that he will be there for us, so we fend for ourselves. We mistakenly think that God is like us. That's why he confronts us in Psalm 50:21 and says, "You thought I was altogether like you."

We think he is like us because that's all we know. We've had others lie to us, change their minds, say things and not follow through and make promises they didn't keep. So we expect God to do the same.

God knows us well. That's why he assures us, "God is not a human being, that he should lie, or a mortal, that he should change his mind. Has he promised, and will he not do it? Has he spoken, and will he not fulfill it?" (Num 23:19 NRSV).

Some of us had parents who were abusive or neglectful. Others had parents who did a decent job but failed to touch the core of our being with acceptance. We came to believe false things about parental love and about ourselves, based on these experiences. We then superimposed those beliefs onto God without even knowing it.

Your Love Broke Through

The year was 1980. I was in my bedroom worshiping God. My prayer life had been steadily growing since my conversion two years earlier. I loved these times with the Lord. I would sing, pray and read the Word. I did the talking and God did the listening. Until today.

As I sat in his presence a thought occurred to me. *You are very special to me. In fact, you are priceless.* I recoiled.

What a bunch of garbage! I heard myself say. *Imagine saying things like that to myself just to feel better!*

I was appalled at my egotism. Suddenly another "thought" broke through: *Are you going to talk yourself out of this or are you going to let me love you?* Only then did I realize what was happening.

"Lord, is that you?"

I had peace in my heart—but also a feeling of discomfort. I knew God loved me in a generic sort of way, but this was intensely personal. Why did this feel so awkward?

Four years later I was sitting at a kitchen table eating my lunch. My new wife was doing some cleaning nearby and listening to a tape of one of our pastor's sermons. He was speaking from Luke 15 about the prodigal son.

"The text says the father saw him while he was a long way off. And he was filled with compassion."

Suddenly a lump started to form in my throat. *What's wrong with me?* I wondered.

"He ran to his son," my pastor continued. "Did you hear that? *He ran.*"

A deep pain began to rise from my insides.

"The father threw his arms around this boy and smothered him with kisses!"

At this point I was out of my chair and literally stumbling toward the couch.

I fell on the sofa and began weeping. Keri rushed to my side and held me in her arms as I shook with convulsive sobs. My pastor continued, cutting me with each word, "Let's have a feast and *celebrate!* For this son of mine was dead and is alive again; he was lost and is found!"

God was speaking to some deep place in my soul. *You are that son, and I do love you!* I cried out many years of accumulated rejection as my wife embraced me, thinking that her husband had finally lost it. But nothing was wrong with me. In fact, something was very right for the first time in my life.

Twelve years later I was on a plane, returning home from a conference in Boston, where I had taught a workshop on depression. I was amazed at how many people had turned out for it, and I was encouraged by their positive response. Teaching at this conference was something of a dream come true for me.

As I looked at the clouds below, I suddenly had a memory. I remembered walking around an industrial complex near my apartment years before. I often went there to pray. When I took these walks, I would see the jets taking off from the airport nearby. As I watched them fly overhead, I always had the same thought: *I wish I were on one of those planes, going somewhere special and doing something important for the Lord.*

I would dismiss this thought and tell myself that flying on a plane and being a speaker wouldn't make me special. Yet I felt an ache in my heart, partly because I wanted it so badly and partly because it seemed so grandiose.

As my thoughts returned to the present and to my seat on the plane, I heard the gentle voice of Jesus say, *You thought that dream of yours was the longing of an insignificant man. You didn't know that it was I who put that in your heart.* Then it hit me. I was experiencing the very fulfillment of that dream. Again his voice broke through, *You thought that was just an example of your pride. You didn't think I loved you enough to give you something so personal, did you, son? What you don't know is that I've waited years to share this moment with you.*

The floodgates of my heart broke open as I leaned my head against the window and wept.

Why do I share these three experiences? Because they demonstrate how my broken past had blinded me to God's loving heart. Because the core of my being had never been adequately touched by either father or mother, I went through life expecting it never to happen. I knew God "loved" me, but I didn't really think he would *nurture* me. Hence my surprise when his words of affection and gestures of kindness confronted me over the years.

The Stingy God

We are so concerned about falling into pride that we are afraid to believe that God would do something special for us, just us. This thinking is not humility; it is actually a misconception of God. We didn't get this idea from the Bible; we got it from adults who were too broken in themselves to celebrate us and mirror our worth back to us in loving words and gestures. Without realizing it, we have sold God short and then tried to let him off the hook by saying, "Well, he doesn't owe me anything."

> **ESSENTIAL FIVE**
> We must explore the origins and content of our perceptions of God. Faulty thinking and responses must be corrected if we hope to develop trust and experience reparenting.

True, he doesn't owe us anything, but he delights in giving good gifts to us (Mt 7:11). He doesn't bless us either spiritually or physically based on our goodness, but based purely on his mercy (Mt 5:45). And though our sin and stubbornness may hinder him, he longs to be gracious and show us compassion, if we'll give him half a chance (Is 30:18). This conditional love that we *think* God is giving us is all in our minds.

What's the evidence that we believe God's love is conditional? Because when we sin, we feel he doesn't want anything to do with us. We feel condemned, worthless and unlovable. This is our way of saying, *God, I know you couldn't possibly love and accept me after what I've done.* This is our hearts talking, not so-called conviction. Didn't the apostle John say that our hearts would condemn us? But God is greater than our hearts and knows we still have worth, regardless of what we think (1 Jn 3:20).

Our sin causes feelings of condemnation for two reasons. First, when we sin we are *supposed* to feel bad. If we didn't, we would have no motivation to change (see 2 Cor 7:9-10). The other reason we feel condemned is that we are accustomed to being rejected or shunned when we do wrong.

This conditioning from our past has a lot to do with our feelings of condemnation today. Sadly, we apply this to God and say to ourselves, "*I know he is disappointed in me.*" No, he is not disappointed with *you.* He is disappointed with your behavior. There is a world of difference.

If we understood this distinction, we would have no trouble coming to God when our behavior demonstrates how sinful we are. Instead, we avoid him at the very time when we most need his throne of grace (see Heb 4:16). This says a lot about how we see him.

God Is Love?

Scripture not only teaches that God is loving, it tells us that he is love personified (1 Jn 4:8). Once again, we say that we believe this, only to return to our pornography and unhealthy relationships. By our behavior we show that we have the same view of God as our non-Christian neighbors: a God who has left us alone in a cold, empty universe.

Most of us have experienced the spectacular love of God at least once or twice. What we don't see is that the God who loved us so powerfully at a retreat or conference still loves us the same way at this very moment. I believe that this too comes from our inconsistent experience of human love.

Many of us were loved by our parents, but by parents who didn't know how to show us beyond the shadow of a doubt that we were priceless to them. For me those times would come when my mother and I were on the open road. This happened once or twice a year when one of her relationships would fall apart and we would travel to another state to live with relatives for awhile.

My little brother would be asleep in the back seat, and Mom and I would talk for hours as we drove through the night. At those times I felt very special as she gave me her complete, undivided attention and warmth. But I knew it was only a matter of time before she would meet another man and be lost to me for another six months or a year.

As children we all relished those times when we had our dad or mom all to ourselves. We enjoyed the fishing, baseball or rare conversation, but many of us knew that was as good as it was going to get.

Now we find ourselves, as adults, believing that God will meet us on special occasions, but think it unreasonable or even selfish to expect that he will love us passionately *all the time*. Naturally we need something to fill up the gaps in between. Hence, our sexual addiction.

God Stands Up

The *real* God, the God of the Bible, is unlike anyone you've ever known. This is how David describes him:

> "The LORD is compassionate and gracious,
>   slow to anger, abounding in love. . . .
> he does not treat us as our sins deserve
>   or repay us according to our iniquities.
> For as high as the heavens are above the earth,
>   so great is his love for those who fear him. (Ps 103:8, 10-11)

David had come to see that nothing he did, no matter how abhorrent, could short-circuit God's love for him.

Does God love only "special" people this way? You know, the ones who read their Bibles, evangelize all the time and never do anything wrong? First, no one exists who fits that description. And second, we are all alike to God. He does not show favoritism (Rom 2:11). The problem is not that God loves some more than others. The problem is that we look at God through the broken lenses of conditional love.

About the time I think I'm beginning to understand the depth of his love, he shows me another side of it. For example, I knew that God loved the church and the Israelites. I also knew that he loved "all those pagans out there." But deep in my heart I didn't believe he loved them the same way.

This belief was exposed one day as I read the book of Isaiah. The sixteenth chapter describes God's judgment on the Moabites. He rebukes them for their "pride and conceit" and says their boasts are empty. Because of their rebellion and demon worship, he is forced to judge them by destroying their impressive vineyards and wiping out their food supply.

Therefore the Moabites wail,
they wail together for Moab. (v. 7)

And then God says,

So I weep, as Jazer weeps,
for the vines of Sibmah.
O Heshbon, O Elealeh,
I drench you with tears! (v. 9).

God is just as broken by their pain as they are. He goes on to say,

My heart laments for Moab like a harp,
my inmost being for Kir Hareseth (v. 11).

This is no vengeful deity meting out disaster to the heathen. This is the heart of a grieving father who is broken over what he must do.

Is this the God you know? One who loves the Christian and the Satanist alike? One whose heart breaks for those sitting in church and for those marching in a gay pride parade? Or does God's love have limits, according to your theology? Do you really believe that God "so loved *the world*"?

You must put aside your beggarly understanding of his love and embrace the fact that he cares for you in a way no one else ever has (see table 2). It doesn't matter what you think about yourself; what does *he* think about you?[1]

Reparenting

Many of us envision a God who is cold and distant. No wonder we seek a warm body to comfort us. It is the only way, in our minds, to fill the parent-shaped hole in our hearts. What we need to do instead is to confront our refusal to trust.

Andrew understood this problem well. His father died when he was ten, and he was reared by a mother who was incapable of intimate relating. Her constant negativity and criticism gradually wore Andrew's self-worth down to nothing. As a young man, he found himself experiencing a hatred of women and, ironically, an insatiable hunger for them as well. This translated into a raging sexual addiction when he became an adult.

Unhealthy view	Healthy view
I'm never sure exactly where I stand with God.	My standing with God is not based on my faithfulness, but on his (Ps 103:10; 130:3; Rom 5:8; 8:1; 1 Jn 3:19-20).
I went too far this time. Now he will let me reap what I've sown.	If I reaped everything I sowed, I would be dead. But God is merciful (sparing me what I deserve) and gracious (giving me what I don't deserve) (Ps 32:1-2; Rom 8:32; 2 Cor 5:19).
This guilt and shame in my heart is God's judgment upon me for acting out sexually. I've brought this misery on myself. I can't expect God to pity me.	God is not "doing a number on me"; my conscience is simply reacting to sin the way it was designed to. God doesn't want to condemn me but give me forgiveness and life (Jn 3:17; 9:10-11; Rom 8:33-34). God is not a harsh father who says, "You've made your bed, now sleep in it!" Regardless of whether we are broken because of *our* sin or painful things that have happened *to* us, he is still deeply compassionate (Ps 31:7; 103:8; 145:8-9; Is 30:15-18; Lk 15:1-2, 11-24).
God doesn't want me to enjoy life and get caught up in "the world." He wants me to serve him and be willing to suffer.	Yes, there is a cross for each follower of Jesus (Mt 16:24). And I must be careful about attaching to this present world. But God made us *human* beings, not merely spirit beings. Hence, he gave me joys and pleasures to relish in this life (Prov 5:18-19; Eccles 2:24; Acts 14:17).
God's number one goal for me is to serve others and evangelize the world.	God's number one goal is to meet my needs and give me life. As I allow him to do this, I will freely serve others out of my fullness (Is 61:1-3; Mt 11:28-29; Jn 10:10; 2 Cor 1:3-4).

Table 2. Contrasts between healthy and unhealthy views of God

It was easy to love Andrew. He had an incredible heart for God. He would literally crisscross whole nations with nothing but a backpack, sharing Jesus Christ with anyone he met. God used him to touch many lives. Unfortunately, his charisma and rugged good looks insured that beautiful girls were always calling or coming over to his house.

After being in our group for a year, he started learning to say no to the constant female attention. This was good, but it caused his inner emptiness to come to the surface. He and I spent many hours in prayer and counseling, working through this new-found agony.

It all hit the fan one night at a Christmas party. I arrived as people were gathering for carols and hot cider. When I walked through the door, I saw Andrew sitting in the corner. His face was red, and it was obvious he had been crying. He gave me one of those "We have to talk" looks. I invited him into another room and closed the door. I asked him what was happening.

"Russ, this might sound stupid, but this is the first Christmas I haven't had a woman by my side. I feel horrible, and I want to run. I know that sex is not the answer, but this is the first time I've chosen to look to God for this and not fall back on what I know."

"Andrew, can we pray and ask the Lord to touch this?"

"I'd like that. But I'll be honest with you, I don't think he can."

"I know. But why don't we give him an opportunity?"

Andrew agreed, and for the next two hours we prayed. His pain made it hard for him to speak, so I did most of the talking. I reminded the Lord that this young man had never experienced safety as a child. His father left him, and his mother was emotionally dead. He had turned to women to quiet the ache in his soul, and that was wrong.

"Yes, Lord," Andrew agreed through his tears.

"The three of us know he can't use women to fill an emptiness that only you can touch. He wants *you* to be the lover of his soul. But he doesn't know how to let you do that. Please come and embrace your son. Enable him to feel the arms of a loving parent right now!"

Andrew broke in, "Lord, I realize that I don't trust you because I see you in the same light as my mother. She did the best she knew, but she was terribly broken herself. Jesus, she didn't know how to love a little boy.

But I'm telling you, Lord, *I will not use women and sex to meet this need anymore!* Even if you do nothing to make this pain go away, I will be faithful to you. Only help me to hold on to you and not go back to what I know."

All of the heartache came out in that moment. I held him in my arms as he sobbed. We both knew that he had turned a corner. No longer was acting out an option for him—even if his heart broke clean in two. From that point on, a new grace was mixed with his pain.

He continued growing and later met a wonderful Christian woman. They have been married for three years now. Though both of them bring deep-seated fears into the relationship, they are learning to love each other.

Conclusion

Your addiction is not only about you and sex; it's about you and God. Like so many, you have seen him through the broken lenses of your past and have imagined that he was "a hard man." Though you may have great faith in other areas (as Andrew did), your faith has been unable to grasp God's nurturing, loving heart toward you.

As you refuse to lump God in with others, your fears will gradually subside. You will find that he is eager to pick you up and hold you, where others have left you to fend for yourself.

8

Reclaiming the Grand Vision

Essential Six:
The Biblical Basis of Our Identity

Peter was impressed by the rabbi. He had already spent time with him a few weeks before and couldn't get the experience out of his mind. Now, in the early morning coolness, a large crowd was gathering by the shore to hear him. As Peter cleaned his nets, he was glad to join the listeners and forget about his wasted night on the lake.

After speaking to the crowd from Peter's boat, the teacher told him to go out for another catch. Peter thought, *Go for a catch? If there's anything out there, it isn't jumping into my nets today. Why don't you stick with preaching and I'll stick with fishing.* Instead, he heard himself saying, "Master, we have worked all night long but have caught nothing. Yet if you say so, I will let down the nets."

Once in the deep water he lowered his nets. He sat there for a moment, thinking that in a short time the teacher would realize there was nothing to be caught. Suddenly the boat lurched to one side. Peter almost fell out. He stared in amazement at his nets. They were beginning to break! What had he snagged? A submerged log, a sunken boat? Then he realized what was in the nets. It was fish.

He and his coworkers began heaving bucketfuls into the boats. This was more fish than any of them had ever seen! In his initial zeal to hoist up all he could, he didn't realize how weighted the boats had become. When he saw what was happening, he yelled out, "Stop, stop! The boats are sinking!"

Suddenly everybody stopped. Nothing could be heard except the sound of water and hundreds of fish flopping at their feet. Only then did Peter realize what was going on: Jesus had done this. When he looked at the teacher, he was overcome with guilt. *Doesn't he know how vulgar and proud I am?* Peter wondered. *If he really knew me, he wouldn't have done this miracle.*

The Master seemed to be looking right through him. It was more than Peter could stand. Falling at Jesus' feet he cried out, "Go away from me, Lord, for I am a sinful man!" Because of his shame and self-hate, Peter wanted to put as much distance as he could between himself and Jesus.

But then he felt a hand pulling his chin up. As he looked up into Jesus' eyes, he saw only kindness. And was that a smile forming on his face? "Do not be afraid," Jesus said. "From now on you will be catching people."

This incident from Luke 5 demonstrates something that every follower of Jesus will have to face: We, like Peter, have a deep sense of self-loathing in our hearts. We can be in denial about this for a lifetime, but the truth will come out the moment the love of God reaches for us and we pull away. This feeling of worthlessness must be worked through in order to diffuse a major source of our sexual addiction. Our sixth essential sums it up: *We must uncover the false beliefs we have about ourselves and deliberately confront them, consistently, with the liberating truths of Scripture. Failure to do this results in psychological defeat and collusion with Satan.*

I am *not* saying that God wants us not to feel bad about our sin. Honest conviction of sin is a good thing—a must. Where we err is in our belief that our sin makes us worthless. In addition to this, we are sometimes tortured by this sense of worthlessness *even when we haven't done anything wrong.* This is the epitome of abandoning shame.

We've already considered how growing up in an abusive or nonaffirming family causes us to see ourselves as less than the diamond God sees. In a moment we will find out what God *really* thinks about us. But first, let's see how our negative self-image sets us up for acting out.

Sex: Pain Relief for the Abandoned Heart

John's years of affairs (as described in chapter one) really had their beginning in his low self-image. He was seeking comfort in the arms of any woman who would affirm his masculinity through her loving attention.

Addictive affairs are a perfect means of falsely addressing this need. They don't carry with them the same reality checks that marriage does. John's wife required that he love her even when she was unlovable. The others never confronted him about his selfishness and immaturity, because they didn't want to lose the relationship.

John's wife made legitimate demands upon him financially, emotionally and spiritually. The others were available for sex whenever John was in town, and then he was free to go with no strings attached. John's wife wasn't afraid to point out his sins, which he mistakenly heard as a reference to his worth. His girlfriends, however, doted on him and told him only what he wanted to hear.

John felt two kinds of shame. He felt ashamed of his affairs, and he felt the shame of unresolved worthlessness from his childhood. To escape, he sought refuge in the very sin that exacerbated his situation in the first place! John's only hope was to find his true worth in someone other than a negative parent, manipulative lover or critical spouse.

Is There No Balm?

John knew his behavior was sinful. He could quote the verses to prove it. But nothing he tried could touch the ache—not his ministry, wife, lovers or superficial theology. When he did turn to others for help, they only rubbed salt in his wounds. I think the Lord had people like John in mind when he said, "Is there no balm in Gilead? Is there no physician there? Why then is there no healing for the wound of my people?" (Jer 8:22).

Many of John's wounds were self-inflicted, to be sure. For those he needed repentance. But for the woundedness behind his immorality he needed understanding. It was an understanding of how God really saw him that finally brought change. God's perspective of you and me is so breathtaking that we can scarcely believe it, but let's give it a try.

Crowned Him with Glory

How does God really feel about you? How would you find out? Obviously the answer is in Scripture. But let me caution you: a part of you will resist what you are about to hear. Years of shaming messages will try to thwart the clear teaching of his Word. But I encourage you to take a risk and dare to believe that what he says is true.

In the beginning we were the crowning glory of God's creation (Ps 8:4-5). He made the earth, wrapped the universe around it and then filled it with vegetation and life (Gen 1:1-25). But when it came to humanity, it was as though he said, "No. This one is different. I will not *speak* this one into being, I will *sculpt* him with my own hands."

And that is exactly what he did. He reached down into the clay and formed the lifeless body with his own fingers. Pulling it close, he placed his mouth over the man's mouth and breathed life into the empty shell (Gen 2:7). Why didn't he create us the way he did everything else? Because we are not like everything else. We have a unique value to him. When God was finished, he looked at the cosmos and the earth—but especially the man and woman—and said his creation was very good (Gen 1:31).

Did Adam and Eve lose this uniqueness after they sinned? Was the divine image rubbed out? Of course not. And if they still bore the mark of eternal love and worth, then so do we. Yet we find ourselves believing otherwise and running to sex to quiet the ache.

Let's go on. How did God approach people throughout history? Was he the vengeful deity that many of us picture? We can easily get this idea when we read of worldwide floods, fire-bombed cities and ruthless armies sent to destroy people. We must keep two things in mind, however. First, these events often had hundreds of years between them. We forget this when we read, in the space of fifteen minutes, about one catastrophe after another. And, second, in every instance God went to great lengths to warn his people to turn from their wicked ways.

After many years of sending one prophet after another, he finally had to act (see Mt 23:34-38; 20:33-43). He could no longer tolerate the child abuse, orgies, human sacrifices and worship of demons. He had to isolate the cancer and destroy it so it wouldn't spread to other nations, thereby requiring another worldwide judgment. So we see that even God's wrath has a loving view to the greater good. This truth is demonstrated most clearly in the sending of his Son, of whom it was said, "It is better for you that one man die for the people than that the whole nation perish" (Jn 11:50).

God has never delighted in judgment. He delights in mercy. He also delights in the men and women he has created. Throughout history God has come to men and women and revealed their specialness to them. And, in almost every case, they had a hard time receiving it.

When he came to Gideon he said, "The LORD is with you, mighty warrior" (Judg 6:12). He said this as the "mighty warrior" was crouching fearfully in a hole to keep the Midianites from seeing him. Gideon asked for sign after sign before he would believe that God's estimation of him was true.

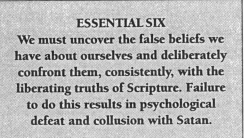

ESSENTIAL SIX
We must uncover the false beliefs we have about ourselves and deliberately confront them, consistently, with the liberating truths of Scripture. Failure to do this results in psychological defeat and collusion with Satan.

When God told Saul he had been chosen as king, Saul had a hard time believing it and said that he was a nobody from a family of nobodies (1 Sam 9:21). He couldn't conceive of God's finding any value in him and asked, "Why do you say such a thing to *me?*"

Hundreds of years later, God spoke to Jeremiah and said, "Before I formed you in the womb I knew you, before you were born I set you apart; I appointed you as a prophet to the nations" (Jer 1:5). Jeremiah was incredulous. His view of himself was so low and his confidence in God's intelligence so small that he said, in effect, "I don't have the skills to do what you ask. Besides I am too young—only a child." Was God impressed by Jeremiah's humility? No. He rebuked him and said, "Do not say, 'I am only a child'" (Jer 1:7).

RECLAIMING THE GRAND VISION

When God speaks forth our value, we tend to resist him. This is not spirituality; it is rebellion. Because we will not let Jesus Christ show us our significance, we persist in finding it through some counterfeit means like sex. We stubbornly refuse his overtures of love and go seeking it in the arms of another woman or in the world of pornography.

Collusion with Satan

Satan knows that if he can get us to see ourselves in a negative light, it is only a matter of time before we sin. This was his tactic in the Garden. He said to Eve, in effect, "God doesn't want you to eat this fruit, because he knows that you will reach your full potential. He doesn't care about you; he's only protecting his own interests. Unlike God, I see the value in you and want you to enjoy life to the fullest!"

Satan was able to convince her that God didn't have her best interest at heart and that he had a clearer picture of her worth than God did. You might think it was ludicrous for Eve to fall for this. But you, as a sex addict, do it all the time. You believe that your new girlfriend, centerfold or act of masturbation will make you feel more valuable than God is capable of making you feel.

Satan's most effective weapon is his attack on our identity and value. He utilized this weapon against Eve, and he uses it against us. The most striking example is his attack on our Lord in the desert. He tried to bring Jesus' downfall by using three primary assaults: he attacked his identity, his calling and his faith in the Father's ability to meet his needs.

Attacked his identity (Mt 4:1-4). "If you are the Son of God . . ." The enemy began by questioning whether Jesus really was who he thought he was. If so, he could "prove" it by turning stones into bread. But the Lord Jesus didn't need to do some parlor trick to establish his identity. He knew who he was.

Do you know who *you* are? Do you find yourself trying to prove you are a son of God by going to church, evangelizing or doing some spiritual thing? If so, you've already taken the bait.

You *are* a child of God right now (see Jn 1:12; 1 Jn 3:1). You don't always act like the royalty you are, but believing that you are less than what God says makes you vulnerable to sin.

Attacked his calling (Mt 4:5-7). "If you are . . . then throw yourself down." Why did Satan take him to the pinnacle of the temple? Because he knew that the Son had been sent to reveal himself to the nation of Israel. What better way than to come flying down out of the sky and land in the temple courts unharmed? Didn't the prophet say, "Then suddenly the Lord you are seeking will come to his temple" (Mal 3:1)? The people would have been astonished and possibly put their faith in him right there. Or so Satan was hoping Jesus would believe.

In effect, Satan was saying, "The people will never put their faith in you if you take the humble route. You need something dramatic and showy. The Father understands your need for publicity and will back you up on this." Jesus saw this ruse for what it was: an appeal to take the ministry into his own hands.

The enemy's tactics haven't changed. He attacks us in this area and tells us that we need to promote ourselves in the church and impress everyone with our spirituality. Otherwise, people will never know how great we are. But God, not Satan, is the source of true self-esteem.

Attacked his faith in the Father's ability (Mt 4:8-10). "All this I will give you." The devil was trying to convince Jesus that he didn't have to go the way of the cross. The Father had said to him, "I will make the nations your inheritance, the ends of the earth your possession" (Ps 2:8). But now the tempter was saying that Jesus didn't have to submit to the Father in order to have this—he could take a shortcut! In other words, "The Father won't give this to you, but *I* will. Just do things my way, and it will be yours!"

Satan comes to us and says the same thing. *You deserve to be loved. But your wife has never understood your needs. This other woman, however, cares for you and will know what a treasure she has in you!* We believe that God cannot meet our deep hunger for love and connection, so we follow Satan's advice and go to a female substitute.

When we do so, it says a lot about how we see God. It also shows how profound is our need to be valued. It is one of the guiding forces of our lives. God knows this and offers himself as the only one who can fill it (see Jn 7:37). Satan, also knowing this, offers a sexual counterfeit.

A Double Bind
I have tried to establish two things: (1) We have a God-given hunger for

value and significance. (2) Contrary to what we may think, God is eager to meet this need.

Many of us have been brought up to believe that seeking personal significance is an exercise in pride. Not only that, the church has reinforced this belief through its "Serve others, forget yourself" mentality. But how can we give to others when we are empty? Are we to use service as a means of filling this need? And if we do, aren't we really serving *ourselves* under the guise of ministry? This puts us in a double bind.

Obviously, we are not to serve others in an attempt to meet our need for self-esteem. Yet we cannot escape our need to feel valuable and worthwhile. So where do we turn? To hear it from some, we can't even turn to God. According to them, we are supposed to meet *his* needs too (this is called "serving the Lord")!

Where, then, can we go to have our needs met? Who will take care of us without expecting something in return? If there is no such place, we are truly alone. No wonder so many of us have turned to sex.

Those of us who seek the answers in Scripture are often frustrated because of the way we've been taught to read them. We've been told that our search for worth and value is condemned by such statements as "Consider others better than you" and "Do not be conceited." Furthermore, we are told to "deny ourselves," not love ourselves. But are we understanding these verses correctly? Does the Bible give us a grand vision or a low self-image?

Grand Vision or Low Self-Image?

The Scripture never uses words like "self-esteem," "self-image" or "positive self-regard." Does this mean the concept is therefore unbiblical? Not necessarily. We don't find "rapture" or "Trinity" in the Bible either. But both concepts are taught throughout.

Let's examine some of the passages that many say contradict the idea of self-worth. We will find out whether the idea of positive self-esteem is a psychological fad or has been a biblical truth all along.

Others better than yourselves. Philippians 2:3-5 says, "Do nothing out of selfish ambition or vain conceit, but in humility consider others better than yourselves. Each of you should look not only to your own interests, but also to the interests of others. Your attitude should be the same as that of Christ Jesus." The way many of us *read* this is: "Don't be ambitious, and remember that others are better than you. Look out for others' interests and ignore your own. Be like Jesus, who served others and never thought of himself."

Fortunately, Paul was not saying this. He said, "Do nothing out of *selfish* ambition." Nothing is wrong with ambition. In fact, both Paul and our Lord were incredibly ambitious. Here is the difference: their ambition was to fulfill God's purposes and build others up. Yet they both experienced great personal joy and satisfaction in doing it (Lk 10:21; 2 Cor 2:3; Phil 2:2; 1 Thess 2:19; Philem 7; Heb 12:2). Joy and satisfaction meet a valid need in us, a need put there by our Creator.

Notice, also, that Paul didn't say others are better than we are. He said, "*Consider* others better than yourselves." We are to treat others with the utmost respect and consideration, but the reality is, we are all equals.

Last, he tells us to be like our Lord, who gave up everything to save us (Phil 2:6-8). Some of us give up everything to serve others and think ourselves very spiritual. But there is one key difference: Jesus knew exactly who he was and emptied himself of his fullness in order to serve. We, however, are often clueless about who we are and attempt to *find* our value and significance through serving. This is giving to *get*, not giving as Jesus did, based on a clear sense of who he was and where he was going (see Jn 13:3-5).

So we see that Paul did not teach that we are of less value in comparison to others. We are of equal value and are supposed to have a clear sense of that; that gives us a healthy base from which to serve.

Do not think more highly. In Romans 12:3 we are told, "For by the grace given me I say to every one of you: Do not think of yourself more highly than you ought, but rather think of yourself with sober judgment, in accordance with the measure of faith God has given you." Many of us interpret this to say, "Don't get a big head, but realize how worthless you really are."

Paul didn't say not to have a high view of ourselves (positive self-esteem); he said not to think of ourselves *more* highly than we should. It is correct to say, "I am of great worth to God. I am unique and supremely loved. My contribution to the body of Christ is as great as anyone else's. I am also capable of the same sin as anyone else." Such a healthy view of ourselves is what Paul was recommending, not the extremes of "I am greater than everyone" or "I am a dirt bag in comparison to others."

Deny yourself. The Lord said in Luke 9:23-25, "If anyone would come after me, he must deny himself and take up his cross daily and follow me. For whoever wants to save his life will lose it, but whoever loses his life for me will save it. What good is it for a man to gain the whole world, and yet lose or forfeit his very self?"

Based on this statement, many of us have been told not to love ourselves but to deny ourselves. There is no question that we are to deny self and obey Jesus. But does this imply that the "self" is inherently bad and must therefore be discarded?

If that's what it means, we have a problem, because the Lord also says, "What good is it for a man to . . . forfeit his very self?" Jesus says that our "very self" has more value than the whole world, and we are not, under any circumstances, to relinquish that part of us.

Now I'm confused. Do we deny and hate the self or do we cherish and protect it? Obviously, there are *two* selves. One is bent on meeting its needs in its own sinful way (this is very relevant to the sex addict). *This* self must be denied and overcome. We are not to give in to its whimpering and pleading. To do so is to come up empty and, in the end, forfeit our lives.

The other self, however, is of great value. We are not to trade it in for anything! That is the self that Jesus died for and to which he wants to give life. Tragically, it is *this* self that we often hate in the name of self-denial!

It is this self that was often shamed by broken parents—the one which we now, in turn, shame and refuse to value the way God does. So, what the Lord is saying is this: that part of you made in my image is of great value and worth. Cherish it, nurture it and bring it into line with the new nature I've put in it. But that part of you that is fallen—kill it without mercy.

The Grand Vision

So we see that God imparts to us a grand vision of our worth. It is ironic to hear atheists, New Agers and secular psychologists talk about having self-esteem, when they have nothing on which to hang that self-esteem!

We, however, have a basis for our self-worth. We have a God who fashioned us with his own loving hands. Who went to painstaking effort to reveal himself to us over thousands of years. Who took on the very humanity we possess. And who then paid the ultimate price to have us as his own.

As if that were not enough, he continues to bless us with material things, miracles without number, and those special touches that only he can give. We have indeed been loved by our God.

Conclusion

You have used sex as an anesthetic to deal with your sense of worthlessness. The only remedy for this is to believe that God sees value in you. You must deliberately and consistently embrace his estimation of you and repudiate your diseased estimation of yourself. Choose not to play along with Satan's attacks on your identity and worth. Cooperate, instead, with the Holy Spirit, and you will see a major plank in the platform of sexual addiction pulled out.

9

- -

The Courage
to Be
Broken

Essential Seven:
*Admitting
Our True State*

Linda was an attractive forty-year-old with four children. Her husband, Stuart, had been the pastor of a thriving evangelical church for eighteen years. She had always prided herself on the "honest" relationship they shared. Unlike other couples, they were able to communicate, laugh and be open with each other. Or so she thought, until she found out about Stuart's seventeen-year addiction to other women.

She and I spent our first few meetings sorting out her feelings of betrayal and grief. It seemed to her that the entire marriage had been a sham. She began to see that her husband was a coward who became what others needed him to be. He found out early in the marriage what Linda expected of him and performed it perfectly. She mistook this for a wonderful relationship.

Linda's upbringing was not pretty. Her father had been a verbally abusive alcoholic. Her mother was extremely controlling and later became addicted to prescription drugs. She spent a lot of time in bed, dealing with various physical and emotional breakdowns and depending on Linda to be the little mother. Linda despised coming from a family that was so "screwed up."

When Linda met Stuart, she thought he was the embodiment of stability and Christian character. She liked being a pastor's wife and reaching out to broken people. Finding out that her husband was one of those broken people was the shock of her life. But the shock wasn't over yet.

"Linda," I said, "it seems really important for you to have a marriage, family and ministry that is 'a cut above.'"

"I thought ours *was*. Now I see that we are as messed up as everyone else."

"Why do you say that?"

"I guess because of what is happening to me. When I first found out about Stuart, I was crushed, of course, but I figured, *Hey, we'll get through this*. But I can't seem to shake this anger and depression. I feel like I should be past this by now."

"Why should you be past this?"

"Because God is with me. I should be able to do all things through him who strengthens me. Instead, I find this self-pity and rage controlling me, and I'm beginning to question whether I am a real Christian or not."

"Real Christians don't *feel* these things?"

"I suppose they do, but *I'm* not supposed to!"

"What do you mean, '*You're* not supposed to'?"

"I know better than this. Jesus has all power in heaven and earth; I should be able to appropriate that and move on."

I could see the problem. "Then, Linda," I asked, "how do you explain Paul's saying that he 'despaired even of life'? Shouldn't he have risen above that? And why did he say that he 'groaned inwardly' and ached for something better? Was he not living the Spirit-filled life?"

Linda looked confused.

"Spiritually speaking," I continued, "Paul was light years ahead of both of us. But he was still broken. Not only that, he was able to admit that brokenness to the whole world. Why can't you do the same?"

"I don't know."

"Could it be that you are terrified of being a mess like your parents?

Could it be that you believed Christianity would deliver you from that and take you to a level where you wouldn't have to struggle with the problems of mere mortals?"

She stifled a nervous laugh.

"The fact is, you are just as broken as the rest of us. Yet being broken is completely unacceptable to you. Jesus wants to show you that you've always been this way. If you can take ownership of your innate weakness, you won't have to 'have it all together.' This will free the Lord to bring into your life the healing that you want so desperately."

Linda's Christianized perfectionism got a cold glass of reality thrown in its face that day. Though it rocked her world, it also began to bring freedom. I have found that grasping our brokenness is absolutely necessary for any person (and especially for sexual addicts) if we hope to experience real change. In fact, it is our seventh essential: *We must grasp our fundamental brokenness and stop pretending we are something else.*

Brokenness Versus Sinfulness

The main reason we struggle with the idea of brokenness is that we see it as a sign of sin. Though the two are related and often overlap, they are not the same thing. What I am calling brokenness, the Lord referred to as spiritual poverty. In fact, he said those who acknowledge their spiritual poverty are blessed (see Mt 5:3).

Unfortunately, most of us cannot admit to such a lack in our lives. It would mean that something was wrong with us. Of course something is wrong with us! That's why we need Jesus.

Through the centuries Christians have been reluctant to admit that they were poor in spirit. To one such group the Lord said, "You say, 'I am rich; I have acquired wealth and do not need a thing.' But you do not realize that you are . . . poor" (Rev 3:17). The fact was that even as Christians they were still in desperate need of him. They just didn't know it. Do you?

David had no problem saying to God, "Hear, O LORD, and answer me, for I am poor and needy" (Ps 86:1). And again, "For I am poor and needy, and my heart is wounded within me" (Ps 109:22). This second statement gives us some insight about brokenness: It comes from being wounded. This wounding can come from being born into a fallen world, being sinned against by others, or committing sins of our own.

Here is why this whole issue of brokenness is so relevant to you: *Your* brokenness may take the form of sexual addiction. I'm not saying you are doomed to act out or fantasize for the rest of your life. In time, and with appropriate accountability, the behavior can cease. What I am saying is that years of abandonment and sinful choices have given your broken state a unique shape. For you, that shape may be of a sexual nature.

Why is this important to understand? Because even when you begin to experience behavioral and internal change, the old system of sexual brokenness will still be intact. It is like living in a house with old wiring. Once new wiring is installed, the house can function the way it was intended. But in our "house" the old wiring occasionally shorts out the new system.

The man who understands this doesn't condemn himself when the old system fires up again. He *expects* such occurrences but quickly defaults to the new settings as soon as he realizes what is happening. However, the man who doesn't understand his fundamental brokenness berates himself when the old machinery kicks into gear. He then falls into self-loathing or says, "What's the use?" and gives in.

Broken Apostles

As mentioned earlier, Paul was light years ahead of most of us. I believe he was one of the greatest servants of Jesus who ever lived. Did he claim to have arrived? Did he represent himself as a man with no further struggles? Let's allow the record to speak for itself: "Not that I have already obtained all this, or have already been made perfect, but I press on to take hold of that for which Christ Jesus took hold of me. Brothers, I do not consider myself yet to have taken hold of it" (Phil 3:12-13). Paul never said that he had arrived.

He did say that he had a single focus and refused to stay stuck in the past. But he was honest enough to admit that his humanness kept him from moving forward perfectly. Not only that, he implied that those who persist in their "all or nothing" perfectionism are immature and need God to teach them further (see Phil 3:15).

He had no problem admitting to the world that he was still a broken man in need of the power of Jesus. He was grieved by his inconsistency and acknowledged his wretchedness (see Rom 7:15, 24).

Some have tried to explain away these statements by saying that Paul was referring to himself prior to his conversion. The fact that we feel the need to explain this away at all says a lot. But Paul was describing himself in the present tense. He says, "Here is a trustworthy saying that deserves full acceptance: Christ Jesus came into the world to save sinners—of whom I am the worst" (1 Tim 1:15). Interestingly, Paul made this statement near the end of his life in one of the last letters he ever wrote.

What about Peter? We all know about his famous denial of Christ. And we've all heard sermons about Peter the coward being transformed into Peter the lion on the day of Pentecost. But that's not where the story ends. We find out in Galatians, chapter two, that he fell into the same sin years later.

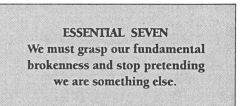

ESSENTIAL SEVEN
We must grasp our fundamental brokenness and stop pretending we are something else.

We're told that Peter had no trouble eating with the Gentile Christians and having fellowship with them. But one day the apostle James and other Jewish believers walked through the door, and Peter made a bee-line for the "kosher" table.

Paul saw what was happening and rebuked Peter to his face for his hypocrisy (Gal 2:11-13). By his actions Peter was saying that Christians have to follow Jewish customs. In effect, this was a renunciation of the grace of God and a denial of Christ (see Gal 2:14-16).

Even as a Spirit-filled apostle, Peter was still vulnerable to this besetting sin. Apparently, he still had a deep brokenness in the area of approval. And this brokenness, though not in itself sinful, led him into sin.

This is exactly the plight of the sex addict. Your unmet need for love and approval makes you vulnerable to sexual compulsion. With time and hard work you can be free of many of the internal and external aspects of the addiction. But the inner deficit will persist—to some degree—until the Lord returns.

Why Be Broken?

You may be wondering what advantage there is to admitting your broken state. Doesn't that just empower the problem, give glory to Satan and keep you stuck in the victim role? The answer is no. The fact is, all of us *are* broken. We have no choice in that matter (see Rom 8:20). We only have two choices: what form our brokenness will take and whether or not we will admit our brokenness.

Before we examine the advantages of admitting our broken state, let's look at the *disadvantages* of pretending. This is what your life as a sex addict will look like if you deny your brokenness:

☐ You will lie constantly for fear that someone will see how "messed up" you are.

☐ You will lead a double life—one that is "Christian" and one that is hidden.

☐ You will get nervous when others discuss sexual immorality.

☐ You will be superspiritual and moralistic in order to throw people off your trail.

☐ You may be liberal and "progressive" because you've given up trying to resist altogether.

☐ You will be superficial in your relationships and be what others want you to be.

☐ You may appear "outgoing" so that others never guess how afraid you are.

☐ You will feel constant guilt about your sexuality.

☐ You may wish that God would remove your sexuality completely.

☐ You will reassure yourself that you are okay except for "this one area."

☐ You will constantly study others, anticipating rejection or disapproval from them.

☐ You will project a false self because the real self is unacceptable to you (and, you assume, to others).

☐ Sometimes you will hate yourself and believe that God hates you.

These are the characteristics of someone who feels the need to "have it all together." He is not free to be who he really is. However, the man who understands the grace of God and admits his broken state has great advantages. If you move in the direction of truth and honesty, this is what your life will look like:

☐ You will not need to hide.

☐ Though you will be concerned about what others think of you, you will not be obsessed with it.

☐ You won't need to "turn on the charm" in order to hide your insecurities.

☐ As you are open to God's acceptance of you, it will change how you see your brokenness.

☐ When you are rejected by others, you will feel pity instead of abandonment, because you will know that they are broken too.

☐ You will seek out other honest people whom you can trust with your brokenness.

☐ When you fall, you will admit it quickly and get back on track.

☐ Better yet, *before* you fall you will reach out and tell someone that you are struggling. (This is impossible if you have to appear to be a "together" Christian.)

☐ You will know that brokenness is a permanent part of the human condition.

☐ You will know that your sexuality is broken and will take time to heal.

☐ You will be gracious toward other broken people instead of critical and self-righteous.

☐ You will publicly share your brokenness (within appropriate bounds), so that others can have hope.

☐ You will know that change, growth, maturity and wholeness are a process, not an event.

☐ You will be patient with yourself but not permissive.

☐ You will live in constant gratitude for a God who accepts you, brokenness and all.

☐ That gratitude—not fear and guilt—will be the motive for your obedience.

Bringing It All Together

As you can see, admitting your inherent brokenness and working through it honestly are essential if you wish to recover from sexual addiction. Though you will, on occasion, despise your brokenness, know that God does not: "A broken and contrite heart, O God, you will not despise" (Ps 51:17). He wants you to understand yourself the way he always has seen you: as a broken man in need of him.

The good news is this: If you will embrace your brokenness, eventually it will not have the power it once did. There was a time when I couldn't go a day without masturbation or compulsive sexual thoughts. Now I stand amazed at the changes the Lord has brought. The thoughts still come occasionally, but I recover quickly and fall into the arms of Jesus. But let me be perfectly clear: *I am not healed.*

Though my brokenness has been deeply touched, it has not ceased to exist. In fact, I had a crisis on a recent New Year's Eve that reminded me of that. Here is my journal entry from that day:

I've been feeling lousy ever since this morning. It started when I went to get gas and saw a cute looking gal filling her tank next to me. I felt that initial pain in my gut but went inside to pay, determined not to dwell on it. When I walked up to the cash register, I was greeted by an even prettier woman.

On any other day I probably would have said, "She's cute," and gone on my way. But not today. This woman was short and beautiful the way my mother used to be. It reached down and grabbed something deep inside me. When I walked back to the car the pain in my gut was worse.

As much as I hate to admit it, I guess there will be times when I still languish over what I don't have on a human level. Keri has grown a great deal, and our sex life has improved dramatically. But I know that what I need cannot be found even in her arms. No, there is only one who can touch this ache.

How I appreciate those touches, Lord! How I cling to the words of life that you speak into my lonely, desperate soul. How I wish there were more of those heart-warming invasions of your splendid grace! Lord, I'm thankful that I don't feel this depression and abandonment very often. That in itself is a great blessing and sign of growth over the years.

Oh, sweet Lord Jesus, what would I do without you? What hope would I have in this world if you weren't the anchor of my life? Sure, I have my beloved, my kids, a ministry that I love and friends who care for me. But in desperate moments like these, who in the universe can possibly understand me like you? "I will be glad and rejoice in your love, for you saw my affliction and knew the anguish of my soul" (Ps 31:7).

Conclusion

Trying to convince yourself and others that you are not broken does not hasten your healing; it hinders it. Be honest the way prophets and apostles were before you. This will disarm the condemning feelings that rise up when you are tempted. Owning the blasphemous twists and turns in your soul will enable you to plow through them with the Spirit's help. This will, after years of hard work, bring you to a place where your brokenness is in the background instead of the forefront.

10

The Unexpected Response

Essential Eight:
*Wrestling
with Grace*

I pulled my chair toward the couch as Diane and Jane sat down. Jane often assisted me when I needed to pray with a female group member, and we definitely needed to pray with Diane.

Diane was Luke's wife. Luke was the one who looked though windows and drove around looking for pornography by the road. Though his acting out had stopped, and though he was treating Diane better than ever, she was still feeling unloved.

Jane spoke up. "Diane, isn't Luke doing better now?"

"Yes, he is. But I still feel unacceptable to him *and* to God."

I suggested we go right to prayer. As we prayed, the picture started becoming clear: Diane felt rejected by a husband who had preferred porn over her. She had felt rejected before that by a drug-addicted boyfriend who beat her and told her she was no good. And before the boyfriend there was a cold and demanding father. It seemed she could never be good enough for any man.

I prayed, "Lord, you know that every man Diane has been with expected her to make the grade. When she didn't, they rejected her. She sees you in the same way: as someone who extends love only when the conditions are met. But, Father, I don't think she has the energy to jump through any more hoops."

Diane began to weep.

I continued, "Lord, show her that you are not like anyone she's ever known. Your love for her is not based on her performance but on your unchanging nature."

Jane agreed. "Loving Father, Diane thinks you need her to obey. What she doesn't know is that you are self-existent—you *have* no needs! When you ask her to obey or trust it is purely for *her* benefit, not yours."

Diane's head jerked with a start and her eyes popped open. "I think I see what you're saying," she said. "There's a difference between God's desire for me to obey and whether he loves me or not."

"Exactly!" Jane and I said almost in unison.

"I've heard about God's grace all my life, but I've never understood it. I have to separate what he is like from what everyone else is like. What you're saying is, he accepts me, *period.*"

"Yes. But that will be hard for you to receive, because no one else has ever treated you that way."

"I think I understand."

Diane turned a corner that day. She and Luke have since graduated from the group and have been instrumental in bringing others to a place of healing. I have yet to work with a sex addict, homosexual or troubled spouse who understands God's grace. They may speak of it with impressive God-talk or teach it to others, but deep in their hearts—where it matters most—it hasn't sunk in. When it does, however, their external and internal lives change.

Our eighth essential is simply this: *We must understand and embrace the grace of God. Otherwise, we will never feel safe in our relationship with him, and we will not have the freedom to fail.*

Why would we want the freedom to fail? Don't we want to succeed? Of course. But all success involves risk. And risk does not take place without occasional failure. For many of us, failure was the one thing we were never allowed as children. We had to dress right, eat right, act right and perform to acceptable standards. As adults, we find this way of relating creeping into our interaction with God.

Ben was seeing prostitutes and visiting massage parlors weekly. Pornography and masturbation were his daily bread. Ben lived with unbelievable guilt. One reason, of course, was his acting out. But he also felt guilt and shame when he *wasn't* acting out.

Ben's father was an authoritarian pastor who drilled into him that God wanted him to be good. The harsh treatment Ben received convinced him that obedience was the condition of God's acceptance. But since he couldn't meet God's "standards," he felt hopeless and defeated and used addictive behavior to comfort himself.

He walked around with a little voice in his head that told him, "You're no good!" Because it was so strong and continuous, he assumed it was the voice of God. I told him that it was neither God nor Satan. It was the deep-seated voice of his dad, expressing itself through his own condemning heart (1 Jn 3:19-20).

We helped Ben retrain his mind (Rom 12:2) and dare to believe that God loved him even when he didn't love himself. Armed with truth and a few supportive men, Ben's beliefs began to change. When he failed, instead of defaulting to his "worthless" setting, he began clinging to the love and grace of God.

In time Ben's addictive behavior diminished as he had a greater and greater desire to respond to one who stood by him no matter what. Ben started to get it. But many of us struggle. Let's look at some of the reasons why God's grace is so hard for us to accept:

☐ We believe it has limits.

☐ The whole idea sounds too easy.

☐ We don't believe that grace is an adequate incentive to holiness.

☐ Since we've never experienced it from anyone else, we cannot conceptualize it.

☐ We know we don't deserve it.

Grace has limits. Doesn't God say, "My spirit will not always strive with man" (Gen 6:3 KJV)? And how do you explain all of those plagues and judgments if not for the fact that God's patience finally snapped?

As we said in chapter seven, God's reason for bringing judgment throughout history was to check the cancer and keep it from spreading. Judgment didn't mean that his grace had been removed. It meant that men and women had hardened their hearts to his grace, and he was compelled to stop them before they influenced others. No matter how wicked an individual or nation may have been, however, God was quick to forgive if only they humbled themselves.[1]

Occasionally our parents disciplined us out of stress or embarrassment. In other words, their discipline (on that occasion) was motivated by *their* need. But God has never done that, because he has no needs. His discipline is strictly for *our* benefit, not his: "Our fathers disciplined us for a little while as they thought best; but God disciplines us for our good, that we may share in his holiness" (Heb 12:10).

God will go to any lengths to make a way for his child. He would even submit to death in order to guarantee you a place by his side: "In him we have redemption through his blood, the forgiveness of sins, in accordance with the riches of God's grace that he lavished on us" (Eph 1:7-8). Does grace have limits? Hardly.

Sounds too easy. Of course it sounds too easy. Nothing in this life is free, and strings are usually attached to the most noble of motives. Again, this is true of humans, not God. Grace might seem easy to us, but it cost him everything. Yet he did it gladly.

I said grace is easy for us, but actually that isn't true; grace is the hardest thing in the world to receive. It goes against everything we've ever experienced. No wonder it sounds too good to be true! So don't try to figure it out—just bask in it.

Inadequate incentive to holiness. I've heard it said that "if you preach all this grace stuff, people won't feel the need to be holy." Guilt and fear might make someone want to be holy (in order to escape judgment), but only love can give someone the *power* to be holy. It may be the slow way, but it is the way that lasts.

Zacchaeus is a good example. As a tax collector he made his money by selling out his own people to the Romans. He also charged more than he was required to, pocketing the difference. The people hated Zacchaeus, and the feeling was mutual.

Then one day he met Love, and it changed his life. What did Jesus do? Did he say, "You know, Zacchaeus, the Bible says . . ."? No, Jesus simply *accepted* him, knowing his flaws perfectly well, and initiated a relationship with him (see Lk 19:1-10).

This grace-filled approach caused Zacchaeus to abandon his immoral behavior. The grace of God has been doing the same thing ever since. It will be grace, not guilt and fear, that will cause you to walk away from your sexual compulsion: "For the grace of God that brings salvation has appeared to all men. It teaches us to say 'No' to ungodliness and worldly passions, and to live self-controlled, upright and godly lives in this present age" (Tit 2:11-12).

Never experienced it from anyone else. This, I believe, is the greatest reason we struggle with the grace of God. We have nothing to compare it to. A few of us had a parent or grandparent who modeled such grace, but most of us didn't. Many have said, "I love you. I'll stand by you to the end"—only to reject us when we fail. This has caused us to ache for a love that is unconditional, but to conclude in our cynicism that that kind of love doesn't exist.

How do we overcome this trap? By memorizing passages or reading more books on grace? Many whom I've counseled have done just that, but with little effect. Understanding grace may involve the accumulation of knowledge, but more than that, it means setting aside our addictive coping mechanisms and letting God help us—*however he chooses to do that.*

Only as we allow him to strip us of our compulsive props do we experience his faithfulness. But first we experience abject terror. Sexual addiction is about attempting to meet emotional needs and avoiding the terror of exposing our core self to God.

We cannot base our understanding of grace on anything that we've experienced in human relationships. Only God can show us what grace looks like. And he will, if we continue to push past our fear and to trust in him.

Aren't deserving of it. Let's settle this right now: *Of course* you aren't deserving of it! And neither am I. "He does not treat us as our sins deserve or repay us according to our iniquities" (Ps 103:10).

We've been taught by a lifetime of experience that we have to earn everything we get. In this world that may be true, but all of that breaks down when it comes to God. He doesn't shower his blessing on us so that we will "owe" him. Others have done that, but Jesus Christ is not like them. Again, he needs nothing that we have. He is self-existent and self-sufficient. He wants only to bless and to give—and we don't know how to handle that!

The best thing you can do is accept his grace even though it goes so badly against your grain. In time you will grow comfortable with it and begin resting. You won't cease to struggle with sexual sin at that point, but you will handle your struggle differently. Instead of obeying in an attempt to silence the guilt, you will obey out of a growing sense of safety in his presence.

Freedom to Fail

I've said that embracing God's grace will give you freedom to fail. Some may be troubled by this, especially when it comes to sexually compulsive behavior. After all, you're not reading this book so that you can fail, but so that you can stop.

True, but here's the point I want to make: whether you extend grace to yourself or hold yourself to a ruthless standard of legalism, *you will still fail.* It is your nature to fail, and God knows that.

I'm not saying you can continue having affairs or soliciting prostitutes. With each contact, you give away a little piece of your soul until there is nothing left. "But whoever commits adultery with a woman lacks understanding: he that does it destroys his own soul" (Prov 6:32 KJV). Nor am I saying you can continue to fuel your masturbatory acts with pornography or fantasizing. These also take a cumulative toll.

In what area, then, are you free to fail? You are free—now don't miss this—to be imperfect. This may sound ridiculous by its obviousness, but it's not as obvious as you think. One of the tactics of Satan is to get us so bound up in doing everything right that every time we fail, we start moving toward giving up.

Let me give an example. Why does a baby learn to walk? Apart from genetic programming, it learns to walk because the parents create a safe environment for it to fail. When the baby loses its footing and topples over, the parents respond by clapping their hands and saying, "Good job! Try again; you can do it!"

The baby is free to make the attempt because he knows he will not be penalized every time he hits the floor. Conversely, the baby who hears, "Can't you do *anything* right?" or "If you do that one more time you're going to *get it!*" will give up trying. The point is clear: in order to learn a new behavior, an atmosphere must exist that allows for failure.

I realize that taking baby steps and trying to stop sexually addictive behavior are not the same thing. But the principle still holds true: we do better under grace than we do under fear.

> **ESSENTIAL EIGHT**
> We must understand and embrace the grace of God. Otherwise, we will never feel safe in our relationship with him, and we will not have the freedom to fail.

If you've turned your back on years of adultery but still masturbate from time to time, you may not be where you want to be, but you must realize *you are not where you were.* You are one more rung up the ladder toward the goal of sexual purity. Keep going, and give yourself grace as you do.

Similarly, if you've been successful at overcoming masturbation but find yourself "rubbernecking," is that okay? No. But realize that you are farther down the road *and God is pleased with your progress.* You should be too.

Work to change the habits and thoughts, but know that it won't happen in a day. You must learn the difficult balance of being uncomfortable with your idolatrous bent, yet not running yourself into the ground for being a fallen creature.

Bringing It All Together

Paul praised the Colossians for bearing fruit and continuing to grow. He said these results came about because the believers "understood God's grace in all its truth" (Col 1:6). This is the key to our growth as well. A mere theological or superficial knowledge just won't do. It makes for enjoyable sermons, but in itself it doesn't change lives. In order to understand the grace of God in all its truth, we have to look at the one who is himself *full* of grace and truth (see Jn 1:14, 17).

How did this personification of grace interact with broken people? More specifically, how did he interact with *sexually* broken people? We could mention many examples, but let's look at Jesus' famous encounter with the woman caught in adultery (Jn 8).

We all know the story, but I don't think we appreciate the amazing implications for our own lives. In fact, the implications are so radical that some theologians have suggested that this account may not have been in the Greek text at all. Since I am not a scholar, I can't comment on that, but I can say that this account is consistent with the Lord's way of dealing with people (including me, I might add).

Can you imagine being caught in the act of copulation and then dragged before Jesus? That is a sex addict's worst nightmare. As the woman stood trembling in fear, the Lord turned his attention to the Pharisees instead. After making quick work of them, he stood up and looked her in the eye. What do think she felt? What did she expect Jesus to say? Whatever it was, this is what she heard:

"Where are they? Has no one condemned you?"

"No one, sir."

Here it comes, she may have thought. *This is where he lowers the boom.* She had messed up and she knew it. And it wasn't the first time. Yet there was something about this man. She didn't see the disgust in his face that she expected. Something in his eyes reached right into her and made her feel both uncomfortable and secure.

"Neither do I condemn you."

What? If the eternal God in human form did not condemn her *or you,* then who is left to condemn you? That's the point—no one! There *is* no condemnation. The only one with the authority to pronounce it has just given you your freedom. This made no sense to her, and it makes no sense to us, but this is the grace of God in all its truth.

When he said, "Leave your life of sin," he wasn't saying, "If you struggle again, I will revoke my grace." "God's gifts and his call are irrevocable" (Rom 11:29). He tells you to leave your life of sin because it is destructive, not because he will abandon you if you don't.

Conclusion

Appreciating God's grace in all its truth will bring the same freedom into your life that it has to others'. Continue resisting the lies: grace has its limits; it's too easy; it can't be true. Remember that, to some degree, failure is a given in your life. But resist the urge to respond to it with either resignation or religiosity. Most of all, remember him who gently tells you to leave your life of sin and promises freedom from condemnation. "For God did not send his Son into the world to condemn the world, but to save the world through him" (Jn 3:17).

11

- -

The
Frightening
Agenda

Essential Nine:
*Facing Our
Dark Side*

_____

"What brings you here?" I asked the handsome man in the suit.

"My pastor suggested I come and see you. I've been involved in several affairs." (I later found out it was eight.) "I know it's wrong, but I've turned my back on all that, and I'm walking the straight and narrow again."

"I'm glad to hear that," I said with hesitation. "But perhaps your pastor felt there were still some issues to work through."

"I'm sure I'm not out of the woods, but other than this part of my life, I'm basically a good person." This distinguished businessman, who had led Bible studies for twenty-five years, was telling me that he was "okay."

"Who told you that you were basically a good person?" I asked.

"Well, I am."

"I thought you were a Bible-believing Christian," I interrupted.

"What's *that* supposed to mean? Of course I'm a Bible-believing Christian."

"Haven't you read where it says: 'There is no one righteous, not even one,' or 'All a man's ways seem innocent to him'?"

He looked at me with a puzzled expression. Obviously he'd forgotten about those verses. Sex addicts tend to have an unbalanced view of themselves. Either they live in perpetual self-hate—which keeps them focused on the problem but not the solution—or they live with a belief in their own moral superiority—in spite of evidence to the contrary. Their behavior actually points to a problem deeper than sexual sin. If you, as a struggler, hope to understand yourself *as you really are,* you must see how deep the cancer goes.

Our ninth essential takes a little courage: *We must come to terms with our personal malevolence and stop assuming our own purity and infallibility.*

Webster defines malevolence as "having or showing a desire to do harm." Though a man may be kind or thoughtful in some areas, he is, at his core, operating out of a desire to meet his own needs no matter whom it harms. In other words, he is malevolent.

Does this sound strong? Am I overstating the case? I don't think so—for three reasons: First, Scripture is very clear about our inherent depravity. Second, my work with sex addicts has confirmed this to me. And, third, I have seen it in my own heart.

When we are confronted with this reality, we respond in one of two ways. We default to our shame and say, "That's right. I'm a worthless dirtbag!" Or we defend ourselves by saying, "I have my problems, but I'm not *all* bad!" Neither response moves us toward truth or healing.

This chapter will be hard for some to read. That is why I've taken such pains to lay a foundation of grace: God's unconditional acceptance of you and those aspects of the addiction that were not necessarily your fault. I hope you've taken those truths to heart. They will give you the courage to read on.

In our attempt to meet the legitimate needs behind our sexual addiction, we routinely hurt those around us. I've spent hours with many a grieving woman as she has poured out her heart over an unfaithful husband. He can never fully appreciate the agony his addiction puts her through. Would to God that every married man would remember this the next time some beauty bats her eyelashes at him.

What many don't understand is that the children feel almost as violated as the spouse. The addict thinks, *This is just between my wife and me.* He is entirely wrong. When his children find out, as they almost always do, their entire foundation is shaken, because fidelity between Dad and Mom *is* the foundation.

Even if we haven't actually been involved with another woman, our wives can sense when we are thinking of someone else even while we are making love to them. I've heard them say, "It was like he was there, but he wasn't there." These flights of fantasy cause the man to be dissatisfied with the woman he married. This dissatisfaction plays itself out in the bedroom and in the rest of the marriage.

It also goes without saying that if we are masturbating in the bathroom, we are depriving our wife down the hall (see 1 Cor 7:3-5). Saying, "I just need more sex than she does," becomes a self-fulfilling prophecy, because masturbation draws his sexual energy away from his wife, causing him to feel less need for her. This is interpreted by her as rejection, which causes her to pull away from him. Prophecy fulfilled.

Infidelity isn't necessary in order for the kids to be damaged. Pornography can do that just fine. I can't tell you how many times I've seen the addictive "baton" passed from one generation to the next as Junior discovers his father's stash. Seeds are planted in his heart that can grow and bear their diabolical fruit years later.

Our addiction harms everyone. Affairs and prostitution hurt women, no matter how willing they may be. After all, what other women need from us is an invitation to follow Christ, not an invitation to go to bed. And every cent spent on pornography maintains a business that must prey on women in order to survive. Are you serving as a redemptive force in society or encouraging its downward spiral into hell?

And what about your brother in Christ? What happens when he finds out about what you are doing? The devil will jump at the chance and whisper in his ear, *If he couldn't resist, what chance do you have?*

Even if no one in the church finds out, the addiction will keep you locked into the false self and prevent you from loving others in a genuine way. It doesn't matter how hard you work in "ministry"; your true self will be hidden away from that brother or sister who hungers for honest friendship.

Our "Uniqueness" and Hidden Agenda

One of the most clever aspects of addictive logic is the tendency to see ourselves as unique. We believe that no one has ever felt the pain we have. Or if he has, he had more strength to deal with it than we have. This is one of the deepest deceptions we face and one of the enemy's most effective ways of keeping us trapped in our addiction. After all, if you are unique in this struggle, others will *have* to make an exception for you. Scripture, however, paints a different picture.

> Be self-controlled and alert. Your enemy the devil prowls around like a roaring lion looking for someone to devour. Resist him, standing firm in your faith, because you know that your brothers throughout the world are undergoing the same kind of sufferings. (1 Pet 5:8-9)

> No temptation has seized you except what is common to man. (1 Cor 10:13)

No matter how strong, constant or lonely your struggle is, you need to know that you are not unique. Other Christians are facing identical battles. Many of them don't have the resources you do, yet they fight on. The ideas that "others are made of stronger stuff" or "no one understands my particular struggle" are lies that keep you right where Satan wants you.

We often perceive that we are unique in our morality as well. We comfort ourselves by clinging to the idea that we are upright in other areas of our lives: "I'm a good father," "At least God uses me at church," or "Thank God I don't believe such and such as *those* people do!"

We also compensate by making strong statements in public against sexual sin, homosexuality, child molestation and abortion. We really are repulsed by some of these, but subconsciously we hope that our grandstanding removes any suspicion that we are struggling with similar perversions.

This whole thing about a subconscious agenda was brought home forcefully to me a few years ago. As I talked with my therapist one day about my latest struggle, I lamented how much I hated this compulsion. Why did I have to struggle in this area? It just wasn't fair! Diane looked at me very calmly and asked, "Russell, do you think you may use your sexual addiction as a security blanket to hide behind?"

Suddenly I realized she was right. I did use my weakness as an excuse. She had exposed me, and until that moment I hadn't even known I was hiding! This also gave me a piece of the puzzle: I "needed" to be an addict. It protected me from letting go of the familiar and moving into the unknown. Now that I saw it, I didn't have to do it anymore.

I left her office feeling exhilarated and hopeful. That day I wrote "Throw off the security blanket" on a card and kept it in my pocket. When the sight of an attractive woman triggered that familiar pain in my heart, I would pull out the card and read it.

That experience taught me something very important about myself, namely, that hidden within my heart was a commitment to hold on to the addiction and protect it at all costs. I was stunned by the deceitfulness of my own heart (Jer 17:9). However, I am no longer surprised when I find evil within. I am surprised only by the clever forms that it takes.

How We Harm Others by Our "Goodness"

When the sex addict says, "If I could only get rid of this problem, then I'd be fine!" I know he is completely blind to his personal malevolence. He doesn't realize that his sexual compulsion is only the tip of the iceberg. He is harming others day after day without even knowing it. It is these harmful interactions with others that form the basis of the addiction.

He is notoriously selfish when it comes to his wife and hurts her without giving it a thought. He rarely loves her as Christ loves the church because he would have to put her needs ahead of his own in order to do that.

He will spend money, pursue a hobby, immerse himself in ministry or give inordinate amounts of time to other relationships without once considering how these affect her. If she complains, he accuses her of being stingy, selfish or "unconcerned about the things of God." These labels are actually descriptions of him.

In the other extreme he may be quick to apologize even when he isn't at fault. When she pushes an agenda that is not in the family's best interest, he won't say anything. Having no clue about healthy boundaries, he feels his only options are to go along or get angry enough to blow up at her. He considers himself a peacemaker. In reality he is a coward, prizing the acceptance of others above their need to be genuinely loved.

He may be a neglectful father whose children take a back seat to his job, ministry or pastimes. Or he may be a compliant father who spends time with them but does so to meet his own needs. In the name of loving them, he actually uses them in an emotionally incestuous way.

Allow me to use a personal example. My daughter and I were talking in my bedroom one day. When she finished what she was saying, she turned to leave but didn't see the edge of the door and walked right into it.

It hit her squarely in the forehead and left a red impression. As she screamed out in pain, I scooped her up in my arms and began rocking her on my lap. As I held her close she cried out, "Mommy! Mommy! I want Mommy!"

At that moment something strange happened inside me. I had an overwhelming urge to thrust her away and say, "Well, if it's Mommy you want, then go find Mommy!" I felt completely rejected. As I continued holding her and struggling with my feelings, the Lord whispered softly to my heart, *You see, you aren't doing this for her, you are doing this for yourself.*

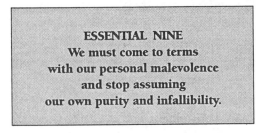

ESSENTIAL NINE
We must come to terms with our personal malevolence and stop assuming our own purity and infallibility.

She was all better in a few minutes and went her merry way. But I was shaken. I couldn't believe that I had done this "loving" action primarily as a way of getting my own nurturing needs met. And by a five-year-old! The Lord had already shown me how selfish my "love" for my wife was. Now I saw that my fathering was not immune either.

If you want Jesus Christ to heal your life, you will have to let him dismantle your perceived goodness. He will do this by allowing the reality of your selfishness to overwhelm your supposed kindness. This will be a painful experience (I can attest to that), but it will enable you to come out of denial and see how dangerous the corridors of your heart really are. This is not the end of you. Believe it or not, this is the beginning of real change and wholeness.

How We Injure God

To me the most chilling aspect of our personal malevolence is how we injure God, and most of us have no idea that we are doing it. I have found that the sex addict does this in four ways: worshiping other gods, rejecting the God he has, blaming God and using God.

Worshiping other gods. It's so easy to dismiss the warning about putting other gods before the Lord. After all, we're not bowing down before some statue, so how could we possibly be guilty of worshiping other gods?

But whenever anything replaces God in our lives, that's idolatry. (We've addressed this somewhat in our discussion about pornography and our tendency to look to others for what only God can supply.)

God says that our constant hunger for sexual gratification is an illustration of our tendency toward idolatry. Listen to this graphic description: "You are a swift she-camel running here and there, a wild donkey accustomed to the desert, sniffing the wind in her craving—in her heat who can restrain her? Any males that pursue her need not tire themselves; at mating time they will find her" (Jer 2:23-24).

This is a perfect description of sexual addiction—the never-ending search for the perfect orgasm. It is so base that God compares it to animals in heat. He pleads with us not to pursue this pattern—but to no avail. "Do not run until your feet are bare and your throat is dry. But you said, 'It's no use! I love foreign gods, and I must go after them'" (Jer 2:25).

Our obsessive longing for porn, women and orgasmic release is not just about sex, it is about the worship of the phallic god. At least the ancients had supernatural beings to worship, grotesque as they were. We, however, have settled for genitals and various bodily functions. As much as this dehumanizes you and me, a far greater tragedy is involved—our abandonment of the glorious God.

Jesus Christ longs to put wonderful things in our outstretched hands, but he can't because we have a death-grip on the addiction. Doing the things we've discussed so far (working through issues, being accountable and so on) are crucial to loosening this grip. It is also crucial, however, to see what our sexual fixation really is: idolatry. If we make excuses for it and do not call it by name, we won't be able to fight its relentless assault.

Rejecting the God we have. When we choose to fantasize about another woman or put our family's needs after our own, we are in clear disobedience to Jesus. He commands us to love our wives without expecting them to reciprocate, which is how he loves us (Eph 5:25). He commands us to meet the nurturing needs of our children. And he requires that we relate to others with openness and honesty.

Our failure to do these things shows not only our weakness of character—it shows that we do not love him: "He who does not love me will not obey my teaching" (Jn 14:24). Our blindness to the evil within prevents us from seeing how small our love for God really is. Love for him is supposed to be demonstrated by submission, not sentimentality.

He comes to us as he did to Peter and asks, "Do you love me?" If we are honest, the only answer we can give is "Not very much." Like Peter's, our denials of Christ prove this. Yet he comes to us and gently exposes our lovelessness so that we can take ownership of it and move on to the real thing.

Blaming God. I am amazed at my ability to blame others for the sins in my life. For instance, I have resented women for the way they dress. If they were more modest, I have reasoned, then I wouldn't struggle so hard. This accusation certainly contains some truth. But it comes dangerously close to my blaming a woman for *my* sin the way that Adam did (see Gen 3:11-12). Not only do we, like Adam, blame women for our failure, but we secretly resent God for making them so gorgeous and us so horny. In other words, all of this is God's fault!

James has something interesting to say about this: "When tempted, no one should say, 'God is tempting me.' For God cannot be tempted by evil, nor does he tempt anyone; but each one is tempted when, by his own evil desire, he is dragged away and enticed" (Jas 1:13-14).

So much for blaming God for what is going on in my heart. Notice also that we can't hang this on the devil. If we feed our sexual drive for years with fantasizing, pornography and acting out, we cannot now accuse God or Satan because we are vulnerable in this area.

Using God. This is the most insidious trait of all: taking the One whose Son bled and died for me and using him to promote my own agenda. But I have found myself doing this very thing. And I have seen others doing it. The clearest example is the Christian leader who uses his authority to seduce someone under his care. It doesn't matter that the other person may have been willing; it is still authority rape.

Another example is the sexually addicted minister who uses the ministry to prop up his fragile ego. Even if he doesn't cross sexual boundaries, he often crosses this one. The pastor, youth leader, missionary or Christian worker who is sexually wounded will tend to use his work with others to meet his own needs for self-worth. Counseling or public speaking become the means of justifying his existence. His significance comes from what he does *for* God rather than from who he is *in* God. That's why he's got to be "busy for the Lord."

I figured out some time ago that my motives for serving God and helping others would never be completely pure. But I take seriously the need to get my self-worth from Christ and not from those to whom I minister. We are supposed to be the donkey upon which Jesus rides into the lives of people, not the other way around.

The "R" Word

How can we possibly respond to all of the treacherous twists and turns of our hearts? Obviously we need others to point them out to us. But even that won't do any good if we aren't open to hearing it. And if we are open, how can we know the truth about our own deceitfulness when our hearts tend to trick us about that as well?

In order to come to a knowledge of the truth about our hearts, we must pursue an ancient practice: repentance. Paul explains it well: "That God will grant them repentance leading them to a knowledge of the truth, and that they will come to their senses and escape from the trap of the devil, who has taken them captive to do his will" (2 Tim 2:25-26).

In other words, what is needed to spot the intrigues of our heart is not necessarily more training seminars, videos or books; it is an attitude of repentance. I call it the "R" word because it is largely meaningless in our evangelical culture.

We often think it means having an emotional experience with guilt and then mustering every ounce of righteous indignation we can to close the door on our sin. Though it may involve this, repentance is what happens *after* that. Do I continue to resist sin in the weeks and months ahead? If I do, I am genuinely repenting.

Repentance is the only antidote I know to the twin evils of closing our eyes to our inherent corruption and lapsing into the shame that says, "I'm no good." Both of these impostors are overcome by a heart that says, "God, I am hopeless without you. Help me now and five minutes from now, when I ask again."

Conclusion

Beneath our sexual addiction is a foundation of deceit and selfishness. This foundation must be exposed and broken up if we wish to change. This inborn malevolence causes us to grieve God, harm others and injure ourselves in ways of which we are not even aware.

This evil is also revealed by our tendency to see our suffering as unique—a view which, in our minds, gives us permission to act out. When we see that our goodness is a farce, we lapse into either a self-pitying shame or a denial of its seriousness. Ongoing repentance is the only honest response and the only effective way of dealing with our dark side.

12

The Hunt
of the
Malnourished
Heart

Essential Ten:
*Dealing with the
Lonely Abuser Within*

I watched her from the darkness. She was wearing gray sweats and doing stretching exercises as she walked. I couldn't understand why an attractive woman would be out here at ten o'clock at night. But here she was, walking around this office building, having no idea that she was being watched from the shadows. *What am I doing?* I wondered. *Am I stalking this woman?*

This had all started several hours earlier. Keri had been abusive in the way she had spoken to our son. She kept going after him again and again: "What's wrong with you, *huh?* Can't you do anything right?" I saw his seven-year-old spirit crumbling beneath her verbal assault.

It was like an instant replay of my own childhood. It made me hurt for him and for myself. I knew what her reaction would be if I spoke to her, but I chanced it anyway. "All right then," she said predictably. "*You* be the parent! Obviously *I* can't do anything right." End of discussion.

My heart ached for my son, my wife and myself. Brandon went to his room, Keri went to the kitchen and I sat on the couch feeling worse by the minute. Depression was wrapping its cruel fingers around my soul. It was hard to breathe.

I have to get out of here! I thought. So I walked out the door and got into my car. I thought the abandoned office might be a good place to pray, so I headed in that direction. After parking, I got out and walked over to the front entrance. It was a two-story building in the middle of a large field. A busy street was nearby, but it was far enough that the people driving by couldn't see me.

I thought there would be a way to get in, but it was locked up tight. As I sat on the ramp, wondering what to do, I was startled by a movement that I glimpsed out of the corner of my eye. That's when I saw her for the first time. She was walking around the building in my direction. I froze. When she passed by, I realized that she hadn't seen me. My fear turned to curiosity.

I hungered to have a woman understand and comfort me. In my state of mind even this stranger seemed like a good candidate. I was still too afraid to let her know I was there. She continued to make a circuit around the empty parking lot, oblivious to my presence.

I just stared at her. That's when I realized that something strange and dark was stirring within me. I'd never felt anything like it. The pitch-dark setting allowed me to entertain possibilities that had never before entered my mind.

She began to walk through the field away from the building, and I realized that she was leaving. My fear of stepping over the line was overcome by my abysmal loneliness. I found myself crying out, "Hello! Hello!" hoping that she'd hear—and terrified that she might. She was too far away and walked out of sight.

Suddenly I came to my senses and realized what was happening. In my despair and neediness I had entertained the thought of connecting with an absolute stranger. What if I had? What if she had been frightened? Was I capable of rape? I was in shock at what had almost happened. As I walked back to my car, I was trembling.

A few days later I confessed the whole thing to my therapist and to Keri. Over time my wife and I resolved the issues that set me off in the first place. But I knew that if I was to avoid a situation like that in the future, I had better understand the differences between legitimate pain and my sinful way of dealing with it. That, in fact, is our tenth essential: *We must differentiate between genuine emotional deprivation and the long-standing pattern of sin that obscures it, knowing where one ends and the other begins.* A lifetime of running when things got hot, isolating myself when I felt rejected, and lapsing into my childish self-pity had set me up to stalk a complete stranger. These were the long-standing patterns of sin in my life that obscured the very real pain beneath.

Since then I have learned a lot about the areas of genuine need in the heart of a sex addict. I have also seen the myriad ways in which we deal with them, most of them ineffective. Let's take a look at these needs.

Matters of the Heart

I am not the first to suggest a grouping of needs. Others have done it before me. But my secular counterparts always leave out the greatest need of all: salvation. Without it the satisfaction of all other needs becomes meaningless. Yet, saved or not, we long for several things. We long for nurture, acceptance, security, competence, independence and impact.

Nurture. We've already discussed nurture in some detail. It is essential for young children during their developmental years. If that need is not met in a solid way, its absence creates feelings of abandonment that eventually lead to rage. Paul uses the word "wrath" (Eph 6:4 KJV). We have nurturing needs as adults too. But many of us don't move on to that level of fulfillment, because we are still seeking what we didn't get in childhood.

Acceptance. We were made to be accepted. We search for it all our lives. We will wear funky clothes and do strange things to our hair in order to get it. On a more serious note, we will step over all kinds of moral lines if there is a possibility that acceptance waits on the other side.

Yet God himself offers acceptance and commands us to extend it to each other as well (see Rom 15:7). When this need is not met it creates great pain. I read recently of a twelve-year-old boy who longed so desperately to be accepted by his peers that he hanged himself when they mocked him for his obesity.

Security. The search for security is a search for *attachment.* The sex addict, however, fears attachment because it has often led to abandonment. He solves this dilemma (in his mind) by forming an unhealthy attachment to sex, rather than a healthy attachment to a person.

Of course, this behavior defeats the whole purpose of sex. Through acting out, he experiences the "high" that substitutes for real attachment, but his God-given hunger for security goes unfulfilled.

Competence. God made us to be competent. He gave the first man and woman the job of ruling the garden and caring for it (Gen 1:28; 2:15). Being competent at what we do fulfills a God-given drive to "subdue and have dominion."

We often excel in those areas that fit our temperaments but avoid any area that threatens to stretch us in new directions. Have you noticed that God often challenges us to achieve competence in the very area where we feel we lack ability? He doesn't do this to frustrate us, but to give us the desires of our heart.

Some of what we long to accomplish can happen only if we push ourselves in the direction of discomfort. This is threatening, so we find competence in something we *are* good at: acting out. Doing this familiar thing helps us compensate for those areas in which we feel inadequate. It meets a legitimate need in an illegitimate way.

Independence. There is a time for every man to leave the care and safety of his parents and strike out on his own. This is usually done when he starts a family (see Gen 2:24). But the move toward independence begins in early childhood, long before we are old enough to marry.

Wise parents will foster their child's growing sense of independence. They will discipline the child for defiance, but they won't confuse that with the legitimate emergence of independence.

In the families that many of us came from, either we were left to fend for ourselves (a counterfeit for independence) or we were made to submit to arbitrary rules that squashed the healthy sense of self that was trying to appear.

The result is that as adults we seek independence through acting out sexually. When we use porn or immerse ourselves in another relationship, we have a sense of doing something "just for me." This is another reason the sex addict lies to his wife; he sees her as the "mother" trying to curtail his freedom once again.

Impact. As children we had dreams of being firemen, policemen, football players and other such heroes. Why those longings? Because we hungered to make a difference in the world. God put this desire in us. As adults many of us have given up on our dream of making a difference. We have settled for making ends meet and experiencing as much happiness as our limited incomes will allow. But deep inside a voice still says, "You were meant for more than this."

We may take a chance and start our own business or get involved in ministry, in which case we do make a positive impact in the lives of others. And to the degree that we do, we are happy and fulfilled (see Jn 4:34; 6:38; Phil 3:14; 2 Tim 4:7). But to the degree that we miss our God-given destiny, we often act out as a means of masking our disappointment.

We have all experienced some degree of frustration regarding the fulfillment of these legitimate needs (nurture, acceptance, security and so on). In childhood many of us developed ways of trying to satisfy them that were both sinful and ineffective. Table 3 shows these emotional needs and the dysfunctional patterns we have employed to address them. It also shows some God-given ways we can begin fulfilling those needs now.

Emotional need	Sexually addictive ways of addressing it	Other addictive ways of addressing it	Healthy ways of addressing it
Nurture	Masturbation (self-nurturing)	Compulsive eating (attempt to fill the emotional emptiness)	Intimate connection with God
	Obsessive sexual attachment to another person		Intimate connection with same-sex friends
		Oral fixations (smoking, drinking, adult thumbsucking)	Healthy, non-manipulative attachment to spouse
			Healthy self-nurture (sports, hobbies, adequate rest, recreation)

Emotional need	Sexually addictive ways of addressing it	Other addictive ways of addressing it	Healthy ways of addressing it
Acceptance	Being "loved" by a prostitute The counterfeit acceptance offered by women in pornography The affirming, reassuring voice of the phone sex operator Being "welcomed" into the privacy of another person through voyeurism	Being a people-pleaser (addiction to the approval of others) Scrutinizing every word, thought or deed to see how others will react—not whether it is right or honest	Embracing God's unconditional acceptance of you Accepting yourself *in toto* (making changes where necessary but not hating yourself for weaknesses) Daring to show your true self to others you can trust
Security	Obsessive sexual attachment to a spouse, lover or prostitute The dependable and predictable ritual that surrounds acting out (certain people, places, acts) Masturbation ("security" of meeting my own need without having to depend on others)	The dependability of "comfort foods" The predictable escape provided by drugs or alcohol The security of having a muscular or thin body (through obsessive exercise, purging) Workaholism (security through obsessive performance at work)	Security in God's love and unchanging attributes Healthy attachments to those God has placed in my life (knowing they will fail me on occasion) Finding security in the true self/gifts/future that God is causing to emerge Knowing that the world contains both beauty and evil and seeing God in both

Emotional need	Sexually addictive ways of addressing it	Other addictive ways of addressing it	Healthy ways of addressing it
Security (continued)	Fantasizing ("In *this* world everything works out the way I want it to") Pornography ("*These* women never make me feel insecure")	Pefectionism (security through "having all my ducks in a row") People-pleasing (the security of being liked by everyone) Negativism ("I know everything always turns out bad; so I can't be surprised by pain") Religious addiction (finding security in theology, emotion or ritual rather than God)	
Competence	Being good at not getting caught Having skill at seducing others Being the best "lover" to a succession of women	Being able to eat, drink or use more drugs than anyone else ("I can drink anyone under the table!") Being a better worker, thinker, performer, fighter, above-it-all person or Christian than anyone else	Feeling good about your growing abilities or performance without having to compare yourself with others (2 Cor 10:12-13; Gal 6:4) Living up to the healthy goals that God gives you, even if you don't meet everyone else's expectations (Gal 1:10)

Emotional need	Sexually addictive ways of addressing it	Other addictive ways of addressing it	Healthy ways of addressing it
Competence (continued)			Growing in an intimate and stable relationship with God and feeling good about it (Jer 9:24)
			Loving others well—in other words, consistently building them up without ulterior motives (Rom 12:9)
Independence	Feeling autonomous only when acting out	Spending inappropriate amounts of time doing things "for you" (sports, recreation, hobbies, career, ministry)	Being deeply *dependent* on God, which always causes you to be out of step with the status quo (see Mt 7:13-14; Jn 15:19)
	Feeling that sexual behavior is the only "private space" you have	Pursuing beliefs, lifestyles or dress for the purpose of shocking others	Finding out who God is making *you* to be and being faithful to that, even if others do not approve (1 Cor 15:10)
	Delighting in casting off moral or societal restraints when it comes to sexuality	Procrastination ("I'll get to it when I want to!")	Being faithful to Jesus and honest with family members, even if it causes division (see Mt 8:21-22; 10:34-37)
		Passivity ("No one is going to make me do anything")	
		Criminality (refusal to be accountable to anyone)	Pursuing your God-given calling, gifts, talents and interests,

Emotional need	Sexually addictive ways of addressing it	Other addictive ways of addressing it	Healthy ways of addressing it
Independence (continued)			even if others attempt to discourage you or squeeze you into their mold
Impact	Seducing others and bringing them under your control (a distorted attempt to "impact" them)

Acting out in more daring and risky ways (not part of the adrenaline addiction but also address-es the need for excitement, danger) | Controlling others through guilt, manipulation or "sweetness"

Sacrificing family, friends, health, spirituality or integrity in order to "make it big" (in business, minis-try, the arts)

Being a political activitist in a fringe movement or pur-suing legitimate activism in obsessive ways

Making your mark by being a rebel (criminality, anti-social behavior) | Impacting God through intercession for others (see Gen 18:23-33; Ex 32:9-14)

Impacting God by your daring faith (see Mt 8:5-10)

Living out your Christianity in such a way that it moves other people—even if words are not spoken (see Mt 5:16)

Being a radical disciple of Jesus, even if it sets you apart from the "Christian main-stream"

Finding your God-given niche and devel-oping it to the fullest (Eccles 9:10; Col 3:23)

Having the *ultimate* impact: loving a woman and children |

Table 3. Three ways of addressing emotional needs

We cannot address these emotional needs if, on the one hand, we try to kill them and say they are not from God, or, on the other hand, we attempt to fulfill them through some addictive means, sexual or otherwise.

Understanding Lust

The way you define lust will have a lot to do with how you deal with it. If you understand it properly and deal with it on that basis, you will experience freedom. But if your approach is simplistic, you are sure to fail.

I believe what we commonly call lust is made up of five interrelated desires. Figure 3 shows these desires to be (1) unmet developmental needs, (2) unmet spiritual needs, (3) healthy sexual desire, (4) habit and (5) true lust. Lust, therefore, is a combination of relational, spiritual, hormonal, habitual and sinful desires. Let's break these down.

Developmental needs. As we've already seen, legitimate needs for nurture, acceptance and love are supposed to be met during our developmental years. If these needs are not met in the first fifteen years of life, they don't cease to exist; they simply change form.

For instance, the longing for nurture can become an obsession with women's breasts. The need for acceptance can be reinterpreted as a need to be seen and noticed by an attractive female. The underlying hunger for love is very genuine and God-given, but *the new way in which it is directed is not.*

Even if our need for nurture is adequately met in the first decade or so of life, we will still hunger as adults for love and companionship. This hunger, however, will not have the compulsive edge that unmet childhood needs do. And since the fulfillment of these needs is crucial for personality development, they will not go away until they are addressed.

Spiritual needs. As a young Christian I heard a lot about the "God-shaped vacuum." I believe this is an accurate concept. But I was told that when Jesus comes to live in your heart the vacuum is filled. I have since found by experience and careful study that this is not completely true.

Just as the living Father sent me and I live because of the Father, so the one who feeds on me will live because of me. (Jn 6:57)

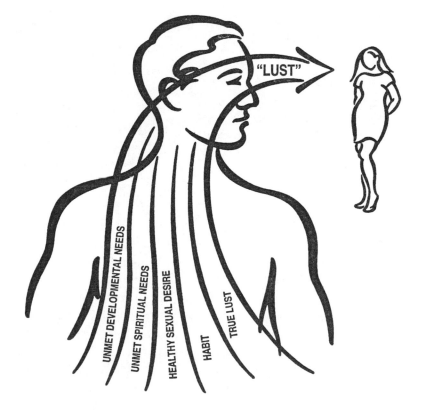

Figure 3. The five components of what we commonly call lust

Notice that the Lord didn't say, "The one who *fed* on me will live." Feeding is a continual experience. The one-time experience of conversion is not enough to meet our ongoing needs. Once he comes to live inside, we must then nurture that indwelling life through ongoing intimacy with him.

Being a Pentecostal, I have also been told that if the new birth didn't take care of the need, speaking in tongues would. I have not found that to be the case either. How thankful I am for all of the Spirit's gifts, but the fact is that even as Christians, our desperate need for God is still ongoing.

> **ESSENTIAL TEN**
> We must differentiate between genuine emotional deprivation and the long-standing pattern of sin that obscures it, knowing where one ends and the other begins.

This "deep calling to deep" (as Psalm 42 describes it) is the soul's cry for connection with the Creator. It is addressed only in his presence. Once satisfied, the need is laid to rest for a short time, only to return once more.

What happens when a Christian does not satisfy this need through ongoing intimacy with God? The need then becomes directed toward something God has made (see Rom 1:25). For the heterosexual male sex addict, this created thing is a woman or a symbolic representation of one.

Benjamin, a lifelong sex addict and missionary, said it this way, "When the loneliness used to hit, I would always turn to the same thing: pornography and masturbation. Now I realize that what I used to call 'loneliness' is actually God calling my name. I see now that the ache in my heart is not a signal to act out, but a reminder that Jesus is knocking at the door." Because Benjamin learned how to open that door, the power of his addiction was eventually broken.

Healthy sexuality. There is nothing unspiritual about sex (contrary to what many of us secretly believe). In fact, all that urgent, sweaty, physical action that takes place in a married couple's bed is called "undefiled" (see Heb 13:4 KJV).

If you are waiting for the day when you become so full of the Spirit that you cease to be sexual, you have a long wait ahead. Sexuality and spirituality are *not* mutually exclusive. In fact, the two are more closely linked than most of us would ever imagine.

Have you ever wondered why God put his special mark on the penis through the rite of circumcision (see Gen 17:9-13)? I believe he was making a statement: "What you do sexually says more about your relationship to me than anything else."

In the New Testament, whenever sanctification is mentioned, sexual purity is never far behind. "It is God's will that you should be sanctified: that you should avoid sexual immorality" (1 Thess 4:3). Why this regular linkage in both Testaments between holiness and sexuality? Because the way we direct our *sexuality* is a definitive statement about our *spirituality*.

The way the church has dealt with sexuality through the centuries has often bordered on attempted murder of the sex drive. But, as Paul taught, our religious rules have no value in restraining sensual indulgence (see Col 3:20-23).

Trying to kill it simply won't work. The most virtuous man who is deliriously happy with his wife will *still* have sexual energy left over. This energy is intended to drive him to the ultimate satisfier of human need: Jesus Christ.

God has put within us a healthy sexual desire. It is strong because it has to be: It helps draw men and women together, affirms and strengthens the marriage bond and produces children. Not only that, but when properly understood it moves us toward God.

This idea of our sexuality being redirected to God is such an important topic that I will devote an entire chapter to it later. Let me just say for now that our sometimes overwhelming drive has a much deeper purpose than marital intercourse.

Habit. The three components of lust we've just outlined are all healthy, God-given desires that are meant to be satisfied. The tricky part is separating them from the unhealthy longings that coil around them. The first unhealthy pattern that must be recognized is habit. Habit is the outgrowth of thousands of undisciplined choices. In time, habit becomes addiction.

The main habits that must be attacked are looking and fantasizing. Though it is natural to notice an attractive woman, the problem is how we look and why. Even the momentary sexual appreciation is normal. It is the cannibalistic stare that must stop. That stare is a habit that can be unlearned.

The bigger problem, however, is the fantasizing that underlies the stare. Fantasizing opens the door to the addictive process. Fantasizing is also a habit that can be unlearned. To understand the incredible power of fantasizing, consider this:

Sow a thought, reap an attitude;
Sow an attitude, reap an action;
Sow an action, reap a habit;
Sow a habit, reap a lifestyle;
Sow a lifestyle, reap a destiny.[1]

No wonder Scripture says, "He who chases fantasies lacks judgment" (Prov 12:11). Unfortunately, many of us have "chased fantasies" for decades, and because of that we're not going to change overnight. We have to continue cutting the legs out from underneath this mental habit. If we persist in this effort, the chemical etching in our brain will begin to reverse.

Nothing thrills me more than to see a sex addict healing in this area. One said to me recently, "I can't believe how much my thinking has changed. At one time I couldn't go a day without aching for sex with another woman. Now I'm seeing a healthy disinterest in other women that is lasting for months at a time."

This man's willingness to look at the issues beneath his pornography and prostitution has produced remarkable internal change. By the power of the Holy Spirit he is growing stronger every day.

True lust. We've examined the underlying components of what is commonly called lust. Now let's look at lust itself. True lust is evil because it is wholly selfish and predatory. The sexual passion that a healthy man feels toward his wife causes him to desire her body, her soul and her pleasure. He has a powerful longing for personal satisfaction, to be sure, but he has learned to subjugate that to the greater priority of bringing joy to her.

True lust is interested not in connection but in gratification. It doesn't care if the other person is sick, powerless, exploited or injured. It will control through seduction, coercion or pity. The person acting out of lust is attempting to fend off his feelings of personal helplessness. Lust itself cannot be reformed. It must be executed without mercy.

Conclusion

You have used sex and other addictive behavior (such as emotional eating or people-pleasing) in an attempt to satisfy your underlying need for nurture, acceptance, security and so on. You have also struggled with lust without realizing the bona fide aspirations it concealed. I hope you have seen the need to deal compassionately with your emotional deprivation, yet ruthlessly with the sinful patterns that surround it.

13

Where
Life & Death
Intersect

Essential Eleven:
Bringing God into
the Area of Need

Keri and I had come a long way in two years. That day by the railroad tracks was a distant memory. And that near catastrophe at the abandoned office was well behind me. I had grown considerably, and we were getting along better than ever. Life was good, and I didn't have to worry about things ever being as they were before—or so I thought. I was not prepared for the abyss into which I was about to stumble.

After getting home from church one Sunday afternoon, we were planning to have sex. Keri put the kids down for a nap and asked if she could rest for awhile first. That was fine with me, so I tried to relax while she slept for the next ninety minutes. Finally, I figured she'd slept long enough and gently woke her.

As she strained to open her eyes, I reminded her that we had planned something other than sleep. She became obviously annoyed and let out a big sigh. As she rolled over on her back she said hatefully, "All right, get it over with!"

There is no way I can explain what happened next. Maybe I expected to be rewarded for letting her sleep. Maybe I expected her to speak affectionately to me. Maybe I thought this could never happen to us again. I don't know. All I do know is that something inside me had the wind knocked out of it. I didn't know if I was going to burst into tears or scream out in rage. What I did instead was to put my clothes on without a word.

I walked out the front door and headed down the street. I wasn't going to drive anywhere, and I certainly wasn't going to do something stupid as I had before. But I had to get away from Keri. I didn't care that people in their cars could see me talking to myself in broad daylight. As I prayed, something strange began to happen. A series of memories began to flash before me. It was as if someone clicked on a VCR and forced me to watch one scene after another.

Scene one. I am five. My brother and I are jumping on the bed and accidentally knock the curtains off the wall. My twenty-one-year-old mother walks in and starts screaming at us. "What's wrong with you kids! Can't you brats keep from tearing this place apart? I'm so *sick* of you f——— brats!" I feel like the worst little boy in the world. Something must really be wrong with me if I can make a grown woman this crazy. No wonder she doesn't love me.

Scene two. I'm sitting under a freeway overpass, crying my eyes out. I am nine years old. My cousin Diane is hiking my little brother on the back of her bike on the roadway.

I have been hopelessly infatuated with Diane for years and she knows it. She would be coy with me one day and cruel the next. Today she is Kenny's "girlfriend" and says, "I'm not going to be your girlfriend anymore!" The two of them laugh at me and ride the bike in circles as I bury my head between my knees and weep.

Scene three. I'm sitting down for dinner with no shirt on. I am fourteen. My mother and I are arguing about something as she carries food from the stove to the table. I smart off and suddenly feel a sharp pain on my bare chest. She has taken a spoonful of mashed potatoes and flung them at me as hard as she can. The look on her face is contempt itself. The scalding potatoes sliding down my chest do not hurt half as badly as the ache in my soul.

Without a word I walk out of the kitchen and into my bedroom. The internal pain is unbearable. I sit on my bed in the darkness and slam my fist against the wall again and again. "God, *I hate you! I hate you!* Why did you even let me be born!" In my misery I curse God, hoping he will kill me and all of this will be over.

These scenes flashed before me, one after the other, as hot tears stung my face. As I cried out to God for relief, the pain only intensified. I felt a suicidal depression that was worse than anything I'd ever known. As the cars whizzed past me, I asked the Lord to make one of them jump the curb and take me out. I meant every word.

It's been years since that experience, and I've had a lot of time to think about it. I realize now that it was a type of post-traumatic stress reaction. I also realize that it was absolutely necessary. I had used everything I could find to protect myself from the loneliness within: girlfriends, acting out, pornography, food and innumerable other escapes. After giving those up, I had used my wife as a protective shield against abandonment.

God knew I hadn't faced the pain. He also knew I was clinging to my wife so I wouldn't have to trust exclusively in him. He knocked both of these false securities out from underneath me in one excruciating blow. The Holy Spirit took years to prepare me for this last invasive procedure, but since that time, my way of dealing with my wife and my sexuality has not been the same.

If you wish to be free, you must let the Lord expose that painful secret area you hide in your heart. As he does so, he will also show you how your compulsive sexual longings actually symbolize your need. This is the very need that Jesus Christ wants to fill. Our eleventh essential is crucial: *We must understand our sexual ritual and the underlying need it symbolizes, learning to meet God and others in this very place.*

We've talked about our *external* ritual: how we use masturbation, pornography and other relationships to keep the pain at bay. Now, let's talk about our *internal* ritual. After all, that is the starting point for everything else. The internal ritual is the inner longing and fantasy that propel us forward in the addiction.

I hope that by this point in your reading, you have gained some mastery over the external ritual with the help of new disciplines, outside account-ability and avoidance of "slippery places." If you are still stumbling regularly, the things I'm about to share may be somewhat premature. I believe they can still be of value, but their greatest benefit will be to those who are now ready to deal with the underlying need.

The Internal Ritual

The internal ritual is that thing your heart does when you are confronted with an attractive woman. For many of us, years of habitual thinking have hardened into an involuntary response. Though you cannot make that response disappear immediately, you *can* deal with the internal ritual, which will cause the involuntary response to reduce gradually to normal levels.

We've already talked about the basis of the involuntary response: unmet developmental needs, unmet spiritual needs, healthy sexual desire, habit and true lust. In order for the internal ritual to lose its power, you must find a way to address all five of these *at the same time.* Christian men do many things in their attempt to deal with this problem. I have probably tried them all. Here are the two most common approaches:

1. *The denial approach.* The denial approach vacillates between two extremes. One says, "I don't have a problem. It's normal to look at other women." The other says, "I *do* have a problem, so I'll just look the other way."

The "I don't have a problem" guys are admitting the reality of healthy sexuality. This is good. But they are going farther than that, and their consciences know it. They are kidding themselves about not having a problem.

The "look the other way" guys are on the right track in that they are changing their habits. But this approach does not deal with the internal longing and implies that something is wrong with the beauty that is woman.

These two denial extremes address some of the needs but leave others untouched. That is why they are unsuccessful in helping us change.

2. *The whistling-in-the-dark-approach.* With this approach, we look the

other way but choose to fill our minds with something else. It is an improvement over the denial approach, which *turns away from* but has nothing to *turn to.* At least we are quoting a verse, singing a song or practicing Scripture memorization; we are filling the vacuum with *something.*

This is a good technique in that it touches on the spiritual need and helps break the lust habit, but it doesn't meet the relational need. We need more than a Christian stop-gap measure. We need something that will address the unmet developmental need.

I know only four ways we can possibly deal with this developmental deficit. One: crawl into a time machine; go back to your childhood and experience the perfect nurturing parents you were intended to have. Two: Use acting out with yourself or others to meet the developmental need. (Yeah, right!) Three: Use your wife as a surrogate mother to meet the needs left by broken parents. (Not recommended. My seven-year experiment with this was a miserable failure.)

That leaves only one alternative: Look to Jesus. Surprised? I didn't think so. But that leads to the $64,000 question: *How* do we let Jesus into this part of us? In order to answer that, we must be both honest and accurate about what that part of us really wants.

What Our Fantasies Mean

Every sexual addict has a recurring fantasy (the internal ritual). However, if he is constantly acting out, he doesn't have time to look behind the obvious scenes of nude bodies and sexual acts. It is the longing behind the erotic symbols that he is actually trying to satisfy.

Jim, the man who would come home from work and masturbate to pornography, was sitting in my office. He had been in our group for six months and had made great strides. The pornography was a thing of the past. But he couldn't shake the obsessive thoughts. I knew it was time to help him see what was really going on. I asked him to be specific about his thoughts.

"Well, I guess you could say I'm a 'breast man.' "

"You mean, when you see a woman's breasts it triggers the thoughts?"

"Yeah. I seem to be obsessed with them."

"It's natural to notice women's breasts, especially the way some women dress. And keep in mind, Jim, that you have years of addictive conditioning working against you. You'll have to be patient with yourself."

"Yeah, I know, but why can't I seem to shake these thoughts?"

"Maybe you haven't taken time to understand what is behind them."

"Do you mean the longing for parental love that we've talked about?"

"Yes. But it's time for you to be more specific about what *this part* of the female anatomy symbolizes to you. What do you think that could be?"

"I've never thought about it before. I just figured I was a pervert who couldn't keep my eyes on a woman's face."

"There's something deeper going on, Jim. Breasts symbolize something for you."

> **ESSENTIAL ELEVEN**
> **We must understand our**
> **sexual ritual and the underlying need**
> **it symbolizes, learning to meet God**
> **and others in this very place.**

"Do you mean like breast-feeding and that sort of thing?"

"Yes. But what is the *emotional* need that this meets?"

"I suppose it would be nurturing."

"Bingo. Breasts symbolize nurture, closeness, warmth, security—all of the things your verbally abusive mother never gave you. Behind the obvious erotic desire is a desire far deeper, one that is, in fact, legitimate. That's why it won't go away. It *can't* until you address it adequately."

Nathan and I had a similar discussion. Nathan was the man who used to cruise for prostitutes after dropping his daughter off at his ex-wife's house. Like Jim, Nathan had stopped acting out but was still troubled by recurring thoughts. I asked him what it was he thought about.

"Well, I can't seem to stop noticing women's rear ends."

"If you want to stop, you're going to have to understand what that part of a woman's body means to you."

"How do I do *that?*" he asked.

"Simple. Tell me what it is you want to do with that part of a woman."

Now he was embarrassed.

"Well, you know."

"No, I don't."

"You're not going to make this easy on me, are you? Okay, I guess my ideal fantasy is to touch that part of her and enjoy it."

"Then what?"

"Are you going to make me break the whole thing down?"

"Only if you want to understand it."

"All right then. I guess at that point I would turn her over and look at her vagina."

"Go on."

"And then I suppose we would have intercourse."

"What is it about intercourse that is so attractive to you?"

"Well, Russ, that's kind of obvious, don't you think?"

"I'm not talking about orgasm. I'm talking about the emotional need that it fills. What do you think that is?"

"Well, I guess I feel accepted."

"So, if a woman welcomes you in that way, it is the ultimate act of acceptance."

"Yeah, I think it is."

"Nathan, you've just identified the real need. The rear end is connected to the vagina. And the vagina symbolizes acceptance. It is acceptance that you hunger for."

"Man, I'd never thought of that before. I think you're onto something."

Our fixation on certain parts of the female body represents a more profound desire. "What a man desires is unfailing love" (Prov 19:22). Yes, we are sexual beings and we have erotic desires. But to the extent that our needs for nurture and affection were not met in childhood, the desires will have power over us now.

Nonsexual Parts of the Body

What if you find yourself smitten by parts of a woman's body that are not obviously sexual, like the arms, legs, face? The issue is still the same, only once removed. In other words, arms and bare shoulders are linked to the breasts, legs to the vagina.

But what about the face? Does the face of an attractive woman capture some unmet need within some of us? Most definitely. The eyes and the mouth have the ability to grab something deep within the soul of the sex addict.

A woman's eyes can signal interest or disinterest, hunger or contempt. The addict also reads things into a certain look that may not be there. But there is no doubt that a woman's eyes are capable of awakening this deep-felt need for acceptance.

The mouth is another example. One day I picked up our Sunday newspaper and started flipping through it. Suddenly I came upon a picture of a rock and roll band that had played a local concert. The picture was of the lead singer's head. She was crooning into the microphone with her mouth in a perfect "O" shape. No bare skin, no lingerie—just a woman's face. But I felt my heart turn to jelly when I saw it. *What is this, Lord?* I asked. *Why does this picture have such an effect on me?*

The Lord reminded me of my constant craving for kissing. (My wife has had to teach me moderation in this area.) Kissing feels very accepting and affectionate to me. My mother was able to kiss me, but I hungered for much more than she was able to give. I saw her kissing other men, devoting her mouth to constant smoking and drinking, and spending hours making her lips even more appealing with lipstick. The mouth definitely symbolizes acceptance to me. And I have found that I am not the only man who feels this way.

The Great Transference
You may be uncomfortable with my frank discussion of bodily parts and functions. It is not my intent to stir up lustful feelings or show disrespect to women by reducing them to anatomy. But sooner or later men are going to have to deal with this honestly. If it's true that these thoughts and longings triggered by the female body have a deeper significance, you won't be able to shake them unless you honestly face what they mean.

How does this knowledge of the female body and its symbolizing of deeper issues help us? It helps by showing us exactly where Jesus Christ needs to make his entrance. The information I'm about to give you is the practical conclusion of everything this book has been moving toward: an intimacy with God that I believe the recovering sex addict is uniquely positioned to experience. I call it the great transference.

Admitting what body part, sexual act or romantic situation you crave is crucial. Identifying the underlying need this symbolizes is more crucial

still. But in order to experience lasting change, you must use this information to move on to the next step. And the next step is intimacy with Jesus.
He wants to be the object of your longing.

The Holy Spirit often uses sexual imagery to explain our relationship
to God. The Song of Solomon is an explicit poem about the king's pleasure
in his wife. But the Lord said that this book also testified of him (see Jn
5:39). The Song of Solomon expresses with passion what Paul expressed
in theological terms in Ephesians 5:31-32 ("The two will become one
flesh." . . . "I am talking about Christ and the church").

In other places the Lord describes his relationship to us, using the
metaphor of attraction, courtship and marriage (see Ezek 16:1-14; Is
54:4-7; Hos 2:14-16, 19-20; Rev 19:6-8). Finally, both John the Baptist and
Paul saw themselves as "best men," as it were, presenting us to our rightful
Lover (see Jn 3:28-29; 2 Cor 11:2).

These sexual images don't make God uncomfortable. And this is where
the recovering sex addict has an advantage. He's already in touch with a
profound need for intimacy and acceptance. The only problem is that he
has confused them with sexuality.

He needs a means of bridging this gap. The great transference is a way
of doing just that. The Lord encouraged at least one sex addict to make
this transference. He told her, in effect, that all of her men and all of her
acting out would never quench the thirst for love within her. But he said
that he could (see Jn 4:10-18).

Obviously the Lord cannot meet our orgasmic need, but he *can* meet
the need behind it, which is obscured by addictive thinking and habit. I
have to be honest with you, though. This is not an easy process. I have
fought it every way I could, and I have looked for every loophole. But in
the end I had to surrender my demand for sexual fulfillment and actively
seek him to touch the ache.

Now, when I see a woman who trips that wire inside of me, I am able
to call it what it is and fall into Jesus' arms. Whether driving down the
street, standing in line at the bank or sitting in church, I am able to reach
out to him. My prayer sounds something like this:

*Lord, I see that woman in the short skirt, and it feels as if her embrace would
love all my pain away. It's a deception. She cannot meet my need for love. My*

*own wife, as affectionate as she is, cannot fill it. Lord, I need YOU. You are the
lover of my soul and the only one who can quench this insatiable thirst of mine.*

*I don't need a woman to wrap herself around me in order to feel loved and
significant—I need your arms. And I thank you, Lord Jesus, that when I come
running to you in my broken, sinful state you wrap those arms around me, just
like the father of the prodigal son.*

*You give me that maternal love that my soul craves. My mother, in her broken
state, failed to nurture me, but you cannot fail! Instead, you say to me, "Can
a mother forget the baby at her breast and have no compassion on the child she
has born? Though she may forget, I will not forget you!" (Is 49:15).*

*O Lord, no one has ever loved me like you. You neither condemn me for
responding sexually to an attractive woman nor allow me to be at peace with
adulterous thoughts. You present yourself to me as the one supreme Nurturer,
whom my soul craves. Thank you for mothering me, caring for me and making
me feel safe. And when I am filled with doubt about your love, I have your
blood to reassure me.*

Broken Mothers/Distant Dads

The most wounded men I have dealt with are those who have experienced
some type of maternal abandonment. One counselee had a mother who
was so broken and angry that she beat him and kicked him repeatedly in
the groin as he curled up under his bed. Others have been wounded by
abusive words or over-control.

Another class of men, however, have had seemingly close and affectionate relationships with their mothers. In many of these cases the mother
was stepping in to "protect" the son from an abusive or neglectful father.
At the very time in his development when he should have been attaching
to his father and laying hold of his emerging masculinity, he was instead
attaching more deeply to his mother. He experienced an affirmation of his
masculinity through identification with a female.

This pattern is not inherently bad, but it often sets the stage for the man
to continue seeking affirmation of his masculinity through female attachment. Pornography, sexual addiction or an obsessive attachment to a
spouse is often the result. Unfortunately, as stated in chapter four, a woman
can call out our masculinity only to a limited degree.

The ultimate challenge to step into your God-given maleness can be made only by another male. That male was supposed to be your father. As adults many men are avoiding healthy and challenging same-sex relationships in favor of the relative safety of a woman's arms (whether physical or pornographic).

Whether your hunger for maternal love has gone unfulfilled (abandonment by the feminine) or been given a suffocating counterfeit (over-identification with the feminine), your need for healthy maternal nurture remains. Though God may use mother surrogates to a degree (wife, grandmother, female therapist and so on), no one can effectively touch this need better than he.

Likening him to a loving mother singing her child to sleep, Zephaniah said, "The LORD your God is with you, he is mighty to save. He will take great delight in you, he will quiet you with his love, he will rejoice over you with singing" (Zeph 3:17). Through Isaiah, God says even more plainly, "As a mother comforts her child, so will I comfort you" (Is 66:13).

Unnecessary Transference?

As I have shared this idea of the great transference with other men, I have heard several objections through the years. One man said, "When I am tempted by another woman, I simply take those thoughts and redirect them toward my wife." Sounds good, doesn't it? But what happens when your wife is in the middle of her period, nursing a headache, feeling emotionally distant or dealing with sexual abuse issues? What if she is in her last uncomfortable weeks of pregnancy, or has recently given birth and is on an emotional roller coaster?

A single man from a Christian college once asked me, "If all of this is true about redirecting our longings to God, what's the point of marriage?" He assumed, like many others, that married sex would fulfill this need. It can to a point, but no woman can fulfill all of a man's sexual desires. He will always have more left over, especially if he is a sex addict.

Another man said to me, "I don't see how talking about body parts and admitting what I want to do sexually with another woman can be a godly way of praying." Yet his mind was *already* populated with naked women, whom he had tried to evict hundreds of times, but who always returned to taunt him and shame him once more.

His mind was stuck in the old addictive track. Only when he learned to embrace what his heart desired—just long enough to use it as a springboard into the presence of Jesus—did he begin to change.

This practice has enabled me and others to "set [our] affections on things above, not on things on the earth" (Col 3:2 KJV). After years of responding in this new way, the process has sped up considerably, enabling me to connect almost immediately with the one whom my soul loves.

The last objection was made by a friend of mine who said, "That's interesting, Russ, but where does repentance come into the picture?" Like many, his idea of repentance was focused on a one-time emotional crisis where we cry out to God, grovel at his feet and then promise not to sin again.

God is more concerned, however, about where we place our focus, not about whether we squeeze out the right emotions: "Let the wicked forsake his way [acting out] and the evil man his thoughts [fantasizing]. Let him turn to the LORD [the great transference], and he will have mercy, and to our God, for he will freely pardon" (Is 55:7).

"Selfish" Praying

Asking God to touch this deficient part of our heart is difficult. But asking him to touch us at all brings up a more basic question: "Shouldn't we be praying for others rather than ourselves? Haven't we been called to serve and to give?" To me, this question betrays lack of understanding about two things: the heart of God and our assumed self-sufficiency.

Our belief that God's primary concern is "what you do for others" betrays our misunderstanding of his heart. This idea doesn't come from him but from questions like, "Hey, kid, do you think the whole universe revolves around you?"

Such childhood training may have been necessary to counteract our selfish bent. But we wrongly concluded from such statements that *our* desires, *our* needs, *our* longings and *our* hopes were of no importance. All that mattered was the good of others.

Nothing could be farther from the truth. *You* matter to God! He didn't come and die for a generic "them." He came for *you*. He invites you to come to him and find rest for your soul (Mt 11:28-30), not "go out and work harder"!

Instead, we tell people from the time they are baby Christians that all that matters is the need of others. This is no different from what they've been told in their dysfunctional families! Yes, we are called to give to others, but we are missing the biblical sequence: "Freely you have received, freely give" (Mt 10:8). I meet believers all the time who have not given themselves permission to get their needs met *first* so that they will have something to offer. When we fall into this trap, we end up using our ministry or addictive behavior to meet our needs rather than our relationship with Jesus.

We do this because we have been taught that our needs don't matter. Yet true ministry always flows from a place of fullness. How can I be full, however, if I am not permitted to go to God for the meeting of my "selfish" needs?

One Christian author whose devotional is read by millions went so far as to say that we shouldn't bother God about our needs at all. And if we are really spiritual, he says, we will quit praying for ourselves.

If this is the proper definition of spirituality, I am not and never have been truly spiritual. I will throw in my lot with David, who basically spent a hundred and fifty chapters bothering God about his needs. I will side with prophets and apostles who were not ashamed to admit they were pathetically empty and in need of God's touch. I will go on seeking him to touch me, heal me and restore me.

Like many children, I did not have the privilege of having an adult who was willing to consistently focus positive attention on me. One who could watch the silly things I did and tell me how "great" I was. One who could find out what I was needing and seek to touch it. My God-given need to be the center of someone's world was never met.

I have had to acknowledge how painful this was. I have had to acknowledge that I used sex to meet my need for specialness. I have also had to acknowledge that my need for specialness is valid (in spite of childhood messages and "Christian" messages to the contrary).

To my great relief and joy, I have found that there *is* someone who is eager to focus on me. He is the only true altruist there is. He demands nothing from me and gives extravagantly without expecting anything in return.

This frees me to come and tell him how lonely, worried, horny or disillusioned I may be. I always find a divine welcome—a fire on the hearth and a warm spot beside him where he waits for me. In that safe and nurturing environment, which for years I didn't believe even existed, he is rebuilding my soul. No one has to tell me now to "go into all the world"—it is my delight to do so. I cannot help but give to others what is being given to me.

Conclusion

We employ every means possible to escape our dark night of the soul. As a sex addict you have used rituals, both external and internal, to do so. You have also used spiritual techniques that may have helped but failed to address all five areas of need. Wholeness will be experienced only as you let go of the sexualized symbols that hide your true loneliness from you.

Be honest about what you want—sinful as it may be—and see that Jesus Christ can meet the underlying need for acceptance and nurture. Actively receiving his positive attention will bring healing to your life. This will empower you to become a healing agent in the lives of others.

14

Boasting in Our Weakness

Essential Twelve:
Radical Honesty &
Its Evangelizing Effect

Andy was a first-time caller. His voice sounded desperate. "I hear that you help sex addicts and homosexuals."

"Yes. Do you struggle in one of those areas?"

"Yes, I do. I'm a Christian and I love Jesus with all my heart, but I struggle with homosexuality and always have."

"Andy, what do you want to do?"

"I want to be free. I have tried everything I know to change, but I still find myself fantasizing about other men. And I hate it!"

After talking for awhile, I found out that Andy had been raised by the emotionally absent father that typifies many homosexual men. I shared with him how this unmet need often becomes eroticized in the form of homosexuality. This made perfect sense to him, but he was deeply troubled about one thing.

"Russell, as a straight man you can't imagine how difficult it is to want something that is inherently wrong—and to want it bad."

"You're right, Andy, I haven't struggled with a life-long desire for men. But I do know what it is like to want something that is wrong, with every fiber of my being."

"Oh? How's that?"

"Since I was a small boy I have hungered for sex with women. I can remember erotic dreams beginning as early as five. It is built into me. In fact, you might call it an 'orientation.' It is an adulterous perversion that I have dealt with all my life."

"Wow, I've never heard a straight guy say things like this. It sounds like you *can* relate."

"Better than you know. But you know what I'm finding? That I can no more look to other women to meet my need than you can look to other men. The same God that mothers me so well can *father* you. No one else is capable of touching your need."

"It sounds like you're talking about a level of relationship with God that I don't know a lot about."

I told Andy that I would be happy to meet with him and discuss it further. Over the next two months he and I explored the differences between the rigid God that he had been raised with (one who "hated" him for his homosexual desires) and the God of the Bible, who was eager to descend into the dark cavern of his soul and deal with the sin and pain.

My relationship with Andy and many others has been paved with admissions of my own brokenness and ongoing restoration. I have also seen how powerfully God uses others who are willing to shed their "perfect Christian" facade and live authentically before the world. This brings us to our last essential. *We must pursue the lifelong work of accountability and honesty in all our relationships and seek to model these values for others. This is evangelism in* its truest form.

Evangelism is not an event; it is a way of life. Many sexually broken men, however, feel they are excluded from this task because of their struggle. If evangelism requires living a perfect Christian life, yes, they are excluded. But if evangelism is a matter of one starving person telling another where to find bread, the recovering sex addict is uniquely qualified.

I believe evangelism flows not only from the words we speak and the tracts we hand out, but from the life we live. God wants to make us a living communique of his truth, "known and read by everybody" (2 Cor 3:2). In order for this to happen, the recovering sex addict will have to continue growing in the areas of personal health, marital health, parental health, relational health and spiritual health.

Personal Health

Addictions tend to come in clusters. It is not uncommon to find someone who is addicted to sex, food, work, spending and a host of other things. Obviously, you have to deal with the most serious addictions first and work your way back. Be patient with this process, but don't use it as an excuse to avoid the other issues indefinitely.

Food. This subject is hard to discuss for several reasons. Number one, it is something I struggle with. Number two, it is socially acceptable in our culture to eat to your heart's delight. Yet you are penalized for being fat (go figure!). And, number three, we Christians have a problem with stuffing our faces that dates back to the potlucks of the early church (see 1 Cor 11:20-22).

The fact that something is acceptable in both the culture and the church doesn't make it right. Likewise, the Scriptures indicate that a problem with food is indicative of deeper issues. The Lord talked about those who would forget about his return and fall into a life of binge eating, drinking and abusing others (see Mt 24:45-51). He said they will be assigned a place "with the hypocrites, where there will be weeping and gnashing of teeth."

You may be one of those who use food to deal with loneliness, depression, stress, fear, boredom or anger. Is that any more effective a solution than buying a pornographic magazine or masturbating? No, it isn't; it's just more socially acceptable.

Food and sexuality are closely linked because you cannot cut them off entirely, as you can smoking or drinking, for instance. You will have to learn the art of eating in healthy ways and not for emotional reasons, just as you are learning to be sexual in healthy ways. For me, utilizing a weight-loss program that emphasizes a balanced diet, exercise and accountability has been very helpful. If this is an area where you struggle, I encourage you to prayerfully seek the accountability and support of others.

Exercise. At the risk of sounding like the Surgeon General, let me say that exercise is important, but not for the reasons you may think. It obviously has physical benefits, but it is also important for emotional reasons. Paul said that "bodily exercise profits little" (1 Tim 4:8 KJV), but he didn't say that it profits nothing.

Many of us spend our days either working, ministering, lying in front of the TV or acting out. We don't have a "private space" that we can call our own. Our relationship with the Lord is supposed to be a big part of this space, but we also need something that is totally unrelated to work, family or ministry.

Because many of us feel guilty about wanting to do something "just for me," we deny ourselves that opportunity. It is this void that acting out often fills. Why not take up racquetball, painting or karate instead of carving out a private space with sexual addiction? Of course, exercise or hobbies can become an unhealthy escape too. Just keep things in balance and glorify God with your body as well as your spirit.

Work. By and large I find that recovering sex addicts tend to overdo it when it comes to their jobs—working sixty and eighty hours a week because they "have to." They do it for lots of reasons: They are unable to draw appropriate boundaries with their boss; work provides an escape from having to relate to their family; work gives them an artificial means of propping up their self-worth; it pays for "the good life."

Work is supposed to be a means of providing for your family, using your abilities to make a mark in the world and living your Christian life before others. But many of us use work, as we have used sex, to meet needs it wasn't designed for. According to Scripture, resting well involves as much discipline as working well. "Let us, therefore, make every effort to enter that rest" (Heb 4:11).

Money. Where there is compulsive sexuality there is often compulsive spending. I'm not saying that you have to give thousands of dollars to missions or the church in order to be spiritual (though it wouldn't hurt some of us). Our attitude and handling of money is the real litmus test.

Do you feel entitled to a certain income? Do you believe that God owes you a middle-class lifestyle? Do you spend money to feel better or elevate your mood? These are questions that are relevant to every believer but especially to someone who has a history of addictive behavior. We in the West are especially vulnerable to the lure of the good life. Our challenge is to enjoy prosperity and graciously accept adversity with equal aplomb (see Phil 4:12-13).

Balanced view of the self. As we've said in chapters eight and nine, we tend to be extremists in this area. We vacillate between seeing ourselves as the center of the universe and seeing ourselves as worthless in comparison to everyone else. The truth is that you are no better or worse than any other person.

At times you will need to get away and take care of yourself in spite of the protest of others. And at other times you'll need to forget about your own needs for the sake of meeting someone else's.

As we have already said, the Lord was a perfect example of this. He could slip away from the crowds to recharge his batteries in prayer or take a nap while others rowed the boat. He could also go without food or rest when it was necessary to help someone else.

As you continue growing away from addiction and closer to Jesus, you will find more of your self-worth being transferred to him and away from human relationships and activities. You will still desire the approval of certain people, but if you fail to get it, you will experience mild disappointment rather than the heart-breaking devastation you once knew.

You will still enjoy a sense of accomplishment from a job well done, but your worth will no longer be contingent upon the job or the fame that comes with it. Your sense of self, though connected with other people and things, will be "hidden with Christ in God" (Col 3:3).

Boundaries. We've emphasized the importance of bringing the physical boundaries back to where they belong. We've also examined the internal boundary violations that we often commit against women. You will need ongoing accountability to keep these boundaries in good repair.

Another area of boundaries that we struggle in relates to seductive behavior. Many of us don't even realize when we are engaged in it. We can be cute, funny, talkative, "sensitive" or flirtatious and not see the inappropriateness of it.

Albert was obviously a "people person," and God used him powerfully. Unfortunately, he had little sense of appropriate boundaries with women.

He had been involved in affairs with two dozen from different churches he had pastored. Fortunately, the acting out stopped, but he still regularly stepped over relational boundaries.

He would be dumbfounded when women accused him of sexual harassment. He just didn't see it. As we worked through the issue of appropriate boundaries, he began to see that he was sending all kinds of signals to women.

I knew he'd gotten the picture when he told me of an experience he had with an attractive young woman. She struck up a conversation as they waited together in line at the Department of Motor Vehicles. After chatting for a moment, Albert realized that he should probably terminate the discussion.

In a friendly voice he said, "It's been good talking to you, but I'm going to turn around and read my newspaper now." Which he promptly did.

People see more of your life than you realize. If you are honoring the Lord in the areas of work, money, self-image and boundaries, they will see that too and be drawn by it. This is the most effective type of evangelism. As St. Francis said, "Preach the gospel by every means available. If necessary, use words."

Marital Health

If you are learning to attach more deeply to Jesus, to be accountable to others and to move toward intimacy, you will begin seeing certain "marks" in your marriage. I call these marks Christ-centered being and wife-centered serving.

Christ-centered being. When I say that our being is to be centered in Christ, I am referring to that part of us that is typically centered in our spouse. We have been brainwashed since childhood to believe that we are supposed to look to our wife to be our all in all.

A thousand movies have told us that everything will fall into place once "boy meets girl." And we have heard sermons and read books that have told us that happiness is found in the ideal Christian family.

We can find great joy in marriage. In fact, as a result of working through my issues, Keri and I have experienced a degree of healing and intimacy that I did not believe possible. A big part of that marital healing, however, came as a result of understanding two seemingly contradictory statements of Scripture.

What I mean, brothers, is that the time is short. From now on those who have wives should live as if they had none. (1 Cor 7:29)

Husbands, love your wives, just as Christ loved the church and gave himself up for her. (Eph 5:25)

Now I'm confused. Am I supposed to love my wife or live as though she doesn't exist?

Both. When it comes to getting *my* needs met, I am supposed to look almost exclusively to Jesus (Christ-centered being). But when it comes to meeting *her* emotional needs, I am commanded to do everything in my power (wife-centered serving). If this sounds difficult, I assure you, it is! Only an anointing of the Holy Spirit will enable you to live in this healthy balance.

Some sexually addicted men are obsessed with private acting out and avoid their wives altogether. For them, moving *toward* their wives in genuine intimacy (both sexual and otherwise) is a tremendous step of maturity and obedience. Others, like me, have used their wives as a sexual and relational feeding trough from which they attempted to fill the bottomless pit in their souls.

All sexual obsession, however, begins with unhealthy emotional dependency. This is the main area where many of us must learn to "live as though we had none."

For the longest time I could not tolerate any gap between my wife and me. If we had an argument, I was quick to make up and apologize, not because I was so spiritual, but because I couldn't stand to be cut off from my one source of identity and being. Somewhere deep inside of me I believed I would die if Keri and I were not soul mates.

God brought this to light one Sunday morning. We had been arguing over something as we tried to get ready for church. Of course, neither of us felt like going then. But I went anyway, even though she decided not to. When I left, things were still unresolved, and I hated how it felt.

It was difficult to worship that morning, but I pushed through it and began to feel God's peace. As I stood in his presence with my brothers and sisters all around me, the Spirit gently spoke, *What do you know, you didn't get everything straightened out with your wife—but you didn't die!*

He said it with a playful sarcasm. I got the point. I would *not* die if Keri and I were disconnected for some reason. I saw that morning that there would be times when I needed to tolerate that distance in order to truly love her the way she needed.

Letting go of my demand that she meet all of my needs—sexual, emotional and relational—has been the most difficult thing I've ever done. It has gone against every fiber of my being and everything I've been taught. But I found, to my surprise, that I was moving toward genuine health. And it took some unfair pressure off of her.

Relinquishing my need for her approval and acceptance has enabled me to be honest even when I knew she wouldn't like it and reach out in love even when I knew she wouldn't reciprocate.

Wife-centered serving. This brings us to the other side of the equation: loving your wife. I don't believe this is even possible until we are prepared to lose them.

I know how strange this sounds, but let me explain. We are to love our wives as Jesus loves us, right? Does Jesus speak and act in our lives based on whether we will like him, or does he do it for our good? If you loved your wife this way, would she always like you?

Obviously God wants you to be a redemptive force in the life of your spouse. But this doesn't mean telling her how to live her life. Women are not the only ones who have to win their spouses over by wordless behavior (see 1 Pet 3:1-2). If your wife is wounded, angry or self-protective, you will have to work very hard to win her trust. This is true in many marriages but especially if you have been unfaithful.

I used to "encourage" my wife by telling her to pray and read her Bible. And I was always so shocked when she was offended by this and dug in her heels. Eventually, God was able to get it through my thick skull that this issue was between her and him. My nagging, well-intentioned as it may have been, only triggered her shame. I began talking less *to* her and praying more *for* her. I prayed for about two years that God would bring revival to her heart.

One day she sat down in the living room and called me over. I could see that something was on her mind. So I knelt in front of her and gave her my attention. Slowly she began to speak.

"I don't know quite how to say this, but I think that God is speaking to me."

"What is he saying to you, baby?" I asked.

"I think he's telling me that I've been asleep."

I was stunned. I had known this for years, but I knew I'd get nowhere if I said it. By God's grace I was smart enough to get out of Jesus' way so that he could say it instead. From that point on I began seeing dramatic changes in my wife. This woman, who had been a Christian for fifteen years but rarely cracked her Bible or prayed, began doing so all the time.

Walls began coming down between her and the Lord. Years of sexual abuse from her childhood and mistreatment at the hands of others began healing as she realized that Jesus was not another abuser.

Something else happened that was completely unexpected: She began to let *me* in as well. She was no longer hearing something critical in everything I said. She was more relaxed around me and more able to communicate. She gradually became able to receive the words of affirmation and praise that I had been saying for some time.

The place where I was most amazed to see these changes was in the bedroom. No longer did I feel despised as a sexual being. Keri began to welcome me and to allow her own God-given sexuality to blossom in a way that I had once despaired of ever seeing.

We have had literal joy as we've bonded sexually. We have learned how to laugh together. We have learned how to share the hopes and dreams of our hearts as well as our secret sins and fears. I can honestly say that I feel completely safe and accepted by her now. But that acceptance, paradoxically, came through my surrender of ever having it.

I am somewhat hesitant to share the joys that my wife and I are experiencing, because I don't want to build false hopes in the minds of anyone. You may not be experiencing this level of transparency and safety with your wife—and may never do so.

You will have to come to the place that I've come to many times—the point where you relinquish your demand of having the perfect, soul-satisfying marriage. God may, at some future date, give it back to you. He may not. If you are truly surrendered, you will be able to accept either.

If you are learning to have a Christ-centered being, you will look to your wife less and less for the meeting of your need for self-worth. At the same time, if you are learning how to affirm her for what she does and who she is and demonstrate that consistently through practical action (wife-centered serving), you will be building her up as God intends.

> **ESSENTIAL TWELVE**
> We must pursue the lifelong work
> of accountability and honesty
> in all our relationships
> and seek to model these values
> for others. This is evangelism
> in *its truest form.*

You will learn to pursue her when there is no prospect of a sexual reward. You will be rubbing her feet, helping her with dishes and entering the world she lives in. You will be taking her face in your hands and looking her in the eyes and saying, "You are a special woman. I'm glad God gave you to me."

And you will love her and seek to connect with her heart even when she is cold, distant, critical or self-protective. In a word, you will be loving her the way Jesus loves and pursues you. In doing this you are revealing the heart of God to your beloved. This is not only good husbanding; it is the way you represent Jesus to your wife.

Parental Health

One of the most exciting things about being a parent, if you are a recovering sex addict, is that you can work through your issues and raise children who are more healthy than you were. One of the most frightening things, however, is that you may not see the ways you are wounding them, because you don't see the wounds in yourself.

The way to avoid wounding your kids is to be sure that you are getting your own needs met by the Lord, in healthy same-sex relationships and, as far as possible, in your marriage. If you are progressing in these areas, you can expect to see the following markers in your parenting.

Nurturing your children. Even if you didn't get the nurturing that God intended you to receive, all is not lost. As we've already said, God can re-parent you and you can then pass on to your children what you are experiencing. This truth is so simple that we often miss it.

I've had zero training and modeling when it comes to being a good father, so I've had to beg God to show me what it looks like. One prime example comes to mind. When my son was four years old, I remember speaking to him about something that he had done wrong. Though I didn't yell, I was very belligerent and rude in the way I did it.

I remember getting into the shower and singing worship songs to the Lord. Suddenly he interrupted me with a question: *Have I ever spoken to you that way?* I had to confess that he never had. *Then don't speak that way to your son.*

After drying off, I found my boy sitting on the couch with his head hanging down. After I apologized to him, he brightened right up. I never want my son, daughter or wife to think that it's okay for me or anyone else to treat them like garbage, because they aren't. They are precious and honored in God's sight (Is 43:4), and I want them to know that they are in mine as well.

I try to speak words of life to them as often as I can. How do I know to do this? Because my mother and father spoke them to me? No. Because Jesus speaks them to me *now,* and I am able to copy him.

I will take my son in my arms at night and pray for him, saying things like, "Lord, thank you for Brandon. He is such a special boy. I love the way he plays soccer, draws comic book characters and tries his best at school.

"I also love the way he laughs, the way he thinks, the way he and I can talk about you. And I love him, Lord, even when he does not obey me or do what I want him to. My love for him and *your* love for him is constant, regardless of whether or not he pulls down straight A's or does everything he's told."

It's a real prayer, but I will phrase it in words a twelve-year-old can understand. I'll do the same for Rachel, my seven-year-old daughter.

And I will say similar things to them as they walk past my chair or ride with me in the car. Because Jesus has gone to such great lengths to show me how valuable I am to him, I have no trouble seeing a similar value in my children and speaking it forth.

Guiding your children. What do you do if you've had very little modeling of how to guide children? Or, worse yet, if your parents were so strict in their guidance that you fear you will damage your kids if you give them similar boundaries? Once again, we have an ace in the hole: our relationship with the Lord.

He guides, but he doesn't push. He sets boundaries, but if we insist on stepping over them, he doesn't insult us and tell us how stupid we are. He lets us suffer the consequences of that choice, then quickly forgives and binds up the wounds when we come running to him in repentance.

Because nurturing was the great lack in my own life, I have tended to err on the side of passivity with my children. I don't yell and scream at them, but I have dropped the ball when I needed to be firm and draw a hard line.

But I'm getting better. I'm learning that they need me to impose certain structures and limits in their lives *that they will hate*. But those limits are crucial if my children are to grow into healthy adults. The reason this is hard for me is that a part of me looks to them for approval and acceptance. When I draw a line I feel like the bad guy, and I'm not their "buddy" anymore.

Those of us who struggle in this area are failing to maintain a Christ-centered being. We are looking to our children, as we have looked to our wives, for love. But aren't we supposed to meet *their* needs instead of using them to meet *ours?* Yes. But we can do that only if we continue looking to the Lord to affirm and satisfy us so that we don't fall into the trap of desperately looking for approval from them.

Providing clear, reasonable boundaries and nurturing their intrinsic, God-given worth are the most important things you can do for your children. Learn to enjoy them; try not to be annoyed with them all the time. Reflect back to them the delight that their true Father feels, and you will be preparing them to enter into a relationship with him. This is good parenting and excellent evangelism.

Relational Health
As I've stressed in chapter four, our need for support and accountability is crucial. We have also discussed the importance of nurturing intimate same-sex relationships that satisfy deep needs for friendship.

Just because you work through your sexual addiction and experience a moderate degree of internal health, you cannot now discard these relationships. If you do, you *will* fall again. You may not fall as far, but you will begin to slip back into old thought patterns and compromises.

If you doubt this, you haven't really understood your own proclivity to sin and self-sufficiency. Keep yourself in honest, open relationships with other men. Let them ask you the hard questions, even if you haven't acted out in years. And let them ask you about the deeper issues that you would rather not discuss. They will keep you from becoming the fool who trusts in himself (Prov 28:26).

You also need levels of friendship. It's okay to have some friends with whom you pray and openly share and other friends with whom you just go to the movies. You need two or three who know everything about you. And you need less intimate friends with whom you can enjoy fishing, football or cookouts.

Don't limit yourself to only a small handful of men. And don't limit yourself only to those men with whom you feel comfortable, either. Someone who is not like you and doesn't agree with all of your political or theological views may be just what you need to challenge you in certain areas.

How about your parents—how do you relate to them as an adult? This is another aspect of relational health. Your parents may still be stuck in their dysfunction. They may still verbally or emotionally abuse you when you are around them. If that is the case, you must learn to draw healthy boundaries with them. You need to do this for three reasons: (1) God does not want you to let anyone demean or belittle you, including your parents. To do so is to renounce your God-given worth and say that Jesus' estimation of you is false. (2) Your parents need to learn that such putdowns are an inappropriate way to treat another adult. (3) You must draw boundaries with your parents or they may mistreat your children as they've mistreated you.

It took me many years before I was willing to talk honestly with my mother about the pain in our lives. I put it off by saying that it would kill her if I told her how I really felt. I also told myself that since she wasn't a Christian, I couldn't be open with her about my addiction and her part in it, because she might be offended—and I was the only "link" she had to God. (No inflated ego there, right?)

Instead of being honest with her, I would avoid her for six and eight months at a time. Naturally, when I did yield to the guilt and pay her a visit, she would open fire as soon as I walked through the door. Her verbal assaults would make me angry, and I'd stay away for another six months, never telling her why it was so painful for me to be with her.

Finally, when I was in prayer one day, God dropped a bombshell on me. *It's time for you to talk with your mother.*

I can't do that, Lord, I protested. *If I do, then we won't have a relationship.*

His answer was direct and to the point: *You don't have a relationship as it is.* I couldn't argue with that. *And furthermore, there can be no relationship in the future unless it is built on truth.*

I knew what I had to do. I went home and began to write a letter detailing all of the things my mother had done, both good and bad, and ended with a list of boundaries that I insisted the two of us agree on—things like no more using guilt as a weapon, no more holding me responsible for your happiness and so on.

A few days later I went to see her and began by asking her forgiveness for my dishonesty and avoidance. I then asked her permission to read the letter. She was kind enough to hear me out. After I had read it, she said, "Do you feel better now that you've got that off your chest?" I felt slightly offended but thought it was better than a nervous breakdown or violent fit on her part.

Since that time things haven't changed much for her. But they've changed incredibly for me. I actually like going over to her house now and spending time with her. I'm accustomed to the smoke-filled environment and the new boyfriends. I've made peace with my mother and her lifestyle and am able now to love her just the way she is. I no longer look to her to be the "mommy" that I needed. I have someone else who provides that for me.

Spending time with others in various levels of relationship not only meets our need for emotional touch but gives us the opportunity to evangelize by the way we live. Neither Christians nor non-Christians need us to protect them from the truth. They need us to live it out and show them that we are just broken people in the process of being healed. Seeing our lives lets them know that it's okay for them to admit their sinfulness and seek Jesus as we do.

Spiritual Health

None of us needs to be told to pray, read our Bible or go to church. These are basics in the Christian life. Yet, because they are basics, they tend to slip away easily. Don't let this happen to you.

Whatever you must do to maintain an ongoing relationship with Jesus—do it! Your recovery from sexual addiction will not continue for long if you neglect your secret time with the Lord. Unfortunately, it is my tendency to neglect this very thing.

But that began to change for me several years ago after I experienced mild burnout. My output exceeded my input, and my upkeep became my downfall, as they say. A friend who loved me cornered me and gently asked how I was doing with the Lord. I told him I wasn't doing real well. He humbly reminded me that the lantern wick would burn out if it wasn't submerged in the oil. This was a clear word from the Lord.

I realized that day that prayer and Bible study were no longer an option for me—they were a *must*. This wasn't a new thought, but it seemed to come with a greater urgency and power. I set out to renew my private life with God.

Through a process of trial and error I found a way of reading through a chapter of Scripture and praying it back to the Lord, applying it to my own needs at the time. This practice has become, for me, a life-changing interaction with God.

It helps me by keeping my Bible study from becoming academic. It has helped considerably to keep me from wandering during prayer. When I do, I just come back to the text. And it has been a means of praying in a way that is unquestionably within God's will.

I also throw in worship choruses and crack open my hymnal from time to time. I will do anything I have to in order to keep my time with God creative and fresh. I must "eat his flesh and drink his blood" regularly or I have no life in me (see Jn 6:53-57). This, by the way, has little to do with the Communion elements, but everything to do with an ongoing "feeding" on Christ.

These times of connecting with him over the last few years have been more powerful than anything else in my Christian experience. I have also had to fight boredom, drowsiness and a host of other distractions, but, by

God's grace, I continue forward.

I encourage you to settle it in your heart to spend vital time with the Lord every week. It doesn't have to be daily, but it does have to be regular. Keep on contending for this "personal space" with Jesus, and the cumulative effect over the years will be transforming.

This too is evangelistic. First, only through an ongoing relationship with the Lord will you have the desire and anointing to live out the gospel in word and deed. Second, if you are not a man of prayer, those you lead to Christ will eventually find that out. They will tend to grow to the level of spirituality that you are at, possibly thinking—as a result of your poor modeling—that serious prayer and Bible study are not necessary. People both inside and outside the church need more from you than that. Seek to be someone they can follow.

Conclusion

In your recovery from sex addiction, *getting* healthy is just the beginning. *Staying* healthy is equally important. This will mean continuing to grow in all areas of your life: personal, marital, parental, relational and spiritual. You must pursue Christ-centered being and, if married, wife-centered serving.

If you put yourself in a position where Jesus can continually nurture you, you will be able to nurture your family in the way that God intended. Your fearless honesty with others, both Christian and non-Christian, will open doors for God to show them their need for him.

Your ongoing accountability and transparency will keep you from falling back into self-deception. They will also serve as a model that others can follow. In fact, this kind of lifestyle is a powerful evangelistic statement that God will use to impact those around you, while he gives you greater and greater freedom from addiction and more and more personal fulfillment through imperfect but genuine relationships.

Postscript

Working Together

We have learned that sexual addiction is powerful, cunning and baffling. It affects not only the spirit but the body as well, right down to the synapses of the brain. All men struggle sexually, but not all men are sexual addicts. For those who are, especially in the church, it is a lonely existence. We can be thankful that this battle is not new to Scripture or to the one of whom Scripture speaks. Jesus Christ has been healing sexually addicted men and women for two thousand years.

The essentials shared in this book are not new. I believe the Holy Spirit has been revealing them to overcomers since the beginning of time. We may have different ways of expressing these truths, whether theological or psychological. But these principles—however we describe them—have been setting people free because they are founded on the eternal Word of God.

My prayer is that the church in the next century will be able to take hold of its God-given ministry to the sexually broken. I believe it is uniquely qualified to do so if it will face its own ambivalence toward the issue. The church is learning to overcome its fear and its judgmental attitude toward the unwed mother, the divorced person, the alcoholic, the drug addict and the gang member. I believe the sexually broken are the last "unreached people group" to be assimilated. They need us to walk alongside them with compassion and understanding, and we can learn to do that even if we haven't struggled in quite the same way.

They need us; we also need them. They have much to teach us about human need, courage and the importance of being ruthlessly honest in a world and a church hungering for reality. There is no greater testimony to the power of the gospel than one person who has come back from the sexual brink. I, for one, am honored to work with those whom God is restoring in this way. Being with them has changed me forever, and I have discovered as I've been in their midst that Another has been there as well. He delights in being among the broken of our church and society as much now as he did when he was criticized for it two thousand years ago. May we not be ashamed to join him.

Appendix A

- -

What Is
a Wife
to Do?

*Help for Spouses
of the Sexually Broken*

I meet with women every week in groups and individual counseling whose husbands are sex addicts. These women are hurting, lonely, confused and angry. Many times the church doesn't know how to help them. They often don't know how to help themselves. The following guidelines have proven useful to many of the women I have worked with. We will look at three areas: working through grief, setting boundaries and dealing with issues.

Working Through Grief

When a woman discovers that her husband is addicted to pornography, videos or other women, her emotional life comes crashing down around her. She experiences several feelings at the same time: shock, betrayal, sadness, fear and anger. She desperately needs to talk with someone about what is happening. But a deep sense of shame makes this difficult. I've heard these women say, "What is wrong with *me*? Why does he have to do *that* to get his needs met?"

These are painful questions, because the spouse of a sex addict usually assumes that her husband's behavior is a result of some lack on her part. "If I were only more interested in sex or lost some weight or tried to be more understanding," she reasons, "then surely he wouldn't be doing this."

What she doesn't understand is that sex addiction is never about the wife, it is about the husband. I'm not saying that she has *no* influence on her husband's behavior; I'm saying that the issue of sexual brokenness is a lot bigger than that. A genuine sex addict is dealing with issues that predate his wife. Therefore, since she is not the cause, she cannot be the cure.

This revelation brings both comfort and pain. Comfort, because the wife finally sees that this is not about her. Pain, because she also sees that she cannot "fix" him and make him all better.

Some women resist the idea that their husband's struggle is not their responsibility. They believe that if they could discover the right key to unlock the door, their spouse would come around.

One woman in our group went on a campaign to win back her sexually addicted husband by performing all kinds of sexual exploits. She did everything her husband asked, even subjecting herself to things that were painful and humiliating. After all this, he was still not satisfied. Only then did she realize that it was not in her power to change him.

Why Is He Like This?

What causes a man to be sexually addicted? Obviously, the first thing is sin, but there is more to it than that. I have counseled those who have fasted, prayed, read the Bible and tried any number of spiritual techniques to rid themselves of the problem—all to no avail.

As I've said before, in my work with sexually broken men I have found a common thread that runs through almost all of their lives: lack of adequate nurturing in early childhood. Sexual addiction is a developmental issue. In other words, something crucial to their development was never put in place.

Outright physical or sexual abuse may have taken place, or the abuse may have been less obvious. Things like verbal put-downs, name-calling, yelling, screaming or distancing on the part of the parent may have caused the child to retreat inwardly and thereby cut himself off from the little nurturing that was available.

This kind of verbal or emotional abuse can be devastating to a child. That is why Scripture says, "The tongue has the power of life and death" (Prov 18:21). Many parents have inadvertently used their tongues to destroy their children's self-worth.

Emotional abuse can also take the form of neglect. This is the hardest type of abuse to identify. When it comes to outright abuse, people usually know if they were physically or sexually assaulted (even though, strangely, they often assume it was their fault). But neglect is harder to pinpoint because we are looking for something that should have been in place but wasn't.

Nine times out of ten, parents who neglect their child's emotional needs do not do it intentionally. They are simply "providing for their family," caught up in their own addiction or unable to give of themselves emotionally because of how they themselves were reared. But to a child who desperately needs Daddy's love and attention, this situation communicates a message: *You are rejected by me.*

Mothers can unknowingly communicate similar messages. Many sexual addicts were brought up in homes where they were required to abide by a number of obsessive rules. In the name of love, some mothers have controlled every action, feeling and experience of their child. If the child didn't keep one of the rules or failed to live up to expectation in some way, the child was made to feel inferior or unaccepted. In homes like this, children learn very early that affection is a reward for obedience. The message is clear: *You have worth only if you obey my rules.*

Early experiences like these in the struggler's childhood taught him that he had no God-given worth and that his value was based on performance. Obviously, if a man's sexual addiction is rooted in his own sinful choices and broken childhood, his wife is not going to be able to fix it through some clever engineering on her part.

The Need to Grieve
Knowing that her husband's sexual brokenness is not about her may bring some initial relief, but it does nothing to soothe the profound ache in her

soul. Whether he has been involved in affairs, anonymous sexual encounters or years of staring at pornography, she will feel deeply violated and betrayed.

No magic formula can remove the terrible sadness in her heart. She will have to feel it and work through it. God understands the need to grieve. In the Old Testament special provision is made for a woman who is taken captive in battle after the loss of her family. God commanded the Israelites to give her time to feel her sorrow and mourn her loss (Deut 21:12-13). The same is needed today.

Two important steps for a wife in this crisis are, first, to give herself permission to mourn and, second, to surround herself with those in the body of Christ who will do the same. The last thing she needs is for some well-meaning Christian to offer her insensitive platitudes, quick fixes or a guilt trip that obligates her to forgive her husband prematurely.

She needs other women who will surround her with love and acceptance and allow her to experience her emotions. She needs to be told it's okay to hurt and to not "have it all together." Unfortunately, she will probably have to work through her grief while shopping for groceries and taking care of kids.

The grieving process has five definite stages: denial, anger, bargaining, despair and acceptance. She will feel all of these at various times and must allow herself to go through the process.

She may display her denial by trying to minimize the situation—pretending it isn't that bad. Whistling a happy tune or "praising the Lord anyway" is not spiritual but, in fact, a means of avoiding the painful truth.

She may bargain by indulging in pornography with her husband or initiating inappropriate sexual activity in an attempt to seduce him away from his "other mistress," sexual addiction.

She may also bargain by doubling her prayer time, Bible study or religious activity in an attempt to manipulate a response from God or her husband.

She will also feel anger as a result of her husband's infidelity or acting out. That is perfectly normal. But staying angry can become a way of hiding from the deeper pain beneath it. Some choose to stay at the anger level because it seems to give them a sense of power and protection, rather than make them feel weak and defenseless.

Inevitably, as she works through the grief process honestly, she will experience the depths of despair, facing the loss of her dream of the perfect marriage. The loss of trust. The loss of control. The loss of faithfulness. While this is anything but pleasant, it is a necessary part of moving on to acceptance.

Coming to terms with the reality of her losses gives way to a true acceptance and ability to forgive, thus allowing her to move forward in a healthy fashion. However, like others who grieve losses, she may go through these stages of grief again and again. She will go in and out of each stage until her heart has emptied itself of its pain. What she needs most is a support network that will give her the space to grieve while loving her enough not to allow her to get stuck.

Setting Boundaries

As she works through her grief, she will also have to set boundaries. A boundary is a nonnegotiable line that lets the other person know that inappropriate sexual behavior or abusive treatment will not be tolerated. It also says that she will not participate in her husband's emotional sickness. Unwillingness to set such boundaries results in codependent behavior that enables the husband to keep on acting out.

A good place to start is to insist that her husband get help. If he chooses not to, this still doesn't give her permission to demand, intimidate or attack. But she must stand by her guns and say: *If you choose not to seek help, I must make some choices of my own.*

Abstinence. The next boundary I recommend is sexual abstinence. I have two reasons for this. First, if there is even the possibility of involvement with someone outside of the marriage, there is a threat of sexually transmitted disease or HIV. In that case, the wife risks her life every time she has sex with him. It is imperative that they both be tested for HIV and refrain from sex until they receive negative test results.

Second, abstinence makes this statement: *If you don't value me and our relationship enough to deal with this issue, I choose not to entrust myself to you sexually.* He can accuse her of controlling and manipulating if he wants to, but the fact is, his choices have forced her to make choices of her own.

Many wives struggle with the idea of refraining from sex because of a misunderstanding of 1 Corinthians 7:4: "The wife does not have authority over her own body, but the husband does." What Paul is saying is that a wife does not have the right to refuse her husband because she is angry, inconsiderate, resentful or selfish. But we are not talking about a situation like that. We are talking about a life-dominating sexual addiction. For the wife to submit sexually to a husband who is actively involved in this kind of behavior is to *encourage* the continuance of his sinful lifestyle.

The wife may give herself to him because
☐ she is lonely
☐ she is taking responsibility for his actions
☐ she is feeling sorry for him
☐ she is being pressed into it by a sense of guilt
☐ she desperately wants to save the marriage

But to do so is not to act in his best interest or her own. When he begins taking responsibility for his actions (and provided there is no threat of STDs or HIV), she can resume the sexual relationship.

Relating Styles

After the sexual boundaries are strengthened, I recommend that some relational boundaries be put in place. These will be harder to implement because they will probably cut to the core of how the couple has related for years. The two codependent relating styles that I've seen most are the avoidant-compliant enabler and the avoidant-persecuting enabler.

The avoidant-compliant enabler. How do some wives enable their husbands to stay sick? First, they refuse to confront. Confrontation is scary, so they avoid it at all costs. Instead of insisting that he get help, drawing sexual boundaries or getting healthy herself, she continues to act as though everything is okay. She denies the obvious, believes she can win him by manipulating his affections or accepts the false guilt that his problem is somehow her fault.

Actually, any response on her part that does not confront the behavior enables the behavior to continue. She must not accept anything short of his stopping all other relationships and all illicit activities. Though he may have occasional relapses at first with pornography or masturbation, she must determine, with the help of experienced counsel, whether each is a minor setback in an honest and diligent recovery process or a demonstration of his insincerity and lack of respect for her boundaries. Her response must be based on that determination.

The avoidant-compliant spouse also fails to hold her husband accountable for his actions. When he says she is to blame for his problem, she accepts it instead of making him responsible for his own choices. When he lies, makes excuses or accuses her of being paranoid, controlling or untrusting, she drops the ball instead of requiring him to be accountable.

Haven't his actions shown that she has every right to be suspicious? Instead she often "goes with the flow" because she believes that is what a godly wife is supposed to do or because she is afraid of losing him. She doesn't understand that there is nothing godly about helping a man continue in his destructive behavior. And, contrary to what she may believe, a sick relationship is *not* better than no relationship at all.

The avoidant-persecuting enabler. The persecutor is stuck in the anger phase of the grieving process. She is never just angry about her husband. She usually has a lot of anger from hurts she has suffered in the past as well.

Her husband's betrayal serves as the focal point for all of her years of unresolved anger. So whenever he fails, even in the slightest, she goes on the attack, making him pay for what he and every other person has ever done to her.

The reason I call her the *avoidant* persecutor is that she uses her anger at her husband to avoid having to deal with her own issues. She makes him responsible for her feelings and feels justified in her resentful response. Like her sexually compulsive husband, she refuses to take responsibility for herself and her emotions, holding *him* completely responsible.

She creates an atmosphere in the relationship where failure of any kind is absolutely unacceptable. She is unconsciously on the lookout for his smallest deviation from her perfectionistic ideal of what he is supposed to be and do. And if she finds it—wham!

Even if he is sincerely trying to change, she will sabotage his recovery by chipping away at his self-worth every chance she gets. This causes him to begin to lose hope and to wonder what the point is of working so hard when his efforts will never be good enough.

She enables his struggle to continue by demanding that he stop his behavior but refusing to be a warm, inviting companion who can replace the addiction he is giving up. She says she wants him to get better, but because of her impossibly high standards she insures that he will fail miserably.

The rare man who is able to move forward in spite of the persecutor's constant attacks is often surprised when she hands him divorce papers just at the time when he is doing his best. She does this because her husband's healing and increasing maturity become an unavoidable contrast to her own unchanging bitterness and inflexibility. In other words, she needs him to stay sick.

The persecuting spouse and the compliant spouse both enable the behavior to continue—they just do it differently. The compliant spouse will put up with almost anything. The persecuting spouse has a very short fuse. The compliant one will allow her husband to be verbally and emotionally abusive. The persecutor draws her guns and opens fire the moment her husband makes a mistake.

Unlike the compliant spouse, the persecutor has a clear sense of boundaries and won't let anyone step over them. Unfortunately, in an attempt to safeguard her own boundaries, she ends up violating everyone else's. The compliant takes care of everyone's needs except her own. The persecutor looks out for "number one" even though someone else's dignity gets destroyed in the process.

The compliant and persecuting spouses are opposite extremes of codependency. And what is codependency? It is an addiction to the approval of others. The compliant needs the approval of others (especially her husband) so badly that she will be whatever he and others want her to be. The persecutor is also desperate for the approval of others; that's why she attacks whenever she doesn't get it.

The compliant must learn to draw boundaries and not be afraid of a fight for the sake of righteousness; the persecutor must learn how to lay down her weapons and begin affirming her spouse and his attempts at recovery.

It will be terrifying for the compliant to meet confrontation head on, because she is afraid of the rejection that she is sure will follow. The persecutor is terrified of affirming others, because she fears that they will take it as a sign of weakness and stop moving toward the goal she envisions for them.

Both must learn to respect their own boundaries and the boundaries of others. And they must value their spiritual and emotional health even more than they value their false security, because, in the long run, that is the only thing that will truly help them or their husbands.

Dealing with Issues

It is hard for many wives to grieve and set boundaries, because they lack inner strength, owing to their fear of abandonment. This is where a woman and her husband are identical. He is holding onto his addiction in an attempt to meet needs and avoid his loneliness. She maintains her unhealthy hold on *him* for the same reasons.

Both have a deep, God-given need for love and are looking to the wrong sources to meet it. When she really understands this, she sees that she is really no better than her husband; they are both idolaters.

The wife must see that her need for love drives her to make choices that actually hurt her and her husband. Her love-need is not bad, but her manipulative ways of trying to secure love are unhealthy. Why is it so hard for her to stop? Because she is broken too.

As she takes an honest look at her own issues, she usually finds that she, like her husband, was raised in a family environment where legitimate emotional needs were not met. Sometimes she was the "little mother" of the family, taking care of siblings, chores and, in some cases, parents. If she perceived that her needs and feelings were not important, she denied her feelings and focused on the needs of others. But spending all of her time being what others wanted her to be insured that her needs for unconditional acceptance and nurture went unmet.

This was perfect training to become the wife of a sex addict. That's why she was able to step right into the caretaking role when he came into the picture. Because she was made to believe her childhood needs didn't matter, and she never learned appropriate boundaries, she is out of touch with her present needs. Consequently, she doesn't know how to communicate honestly or address her needs in healthy ways.

This is why it's so important for her to take a candid look at her own issues. She will need outside support, because she will tend to gloss over pain from her past and not deal with it honestly.

Usually the spouse of a sex addict prides herself on being honest. In reality, she is *dishonest* with herself about her own issues and about the truth regarding her husband. She is also dishonest with others. Instead of telling others the truth, she will say yes when she really wants to say no. Later, when she is groaning beneath the burden of something she agreed to do for someone, she resents *that person,* never realizing that it was her inability to say no that got her into this dilemma in the first place.

Why does she feel this urgency to please everyone? It is because she is terrified of rejection and desperately seeks approval. Just as her husband feels he has worth only when he is sexual, she feels she has worth only when she can *do* something for someone.

She is like Martha, banging pots and pans around in the kitchen and resenting that she has to work so hard for everyone, not realizing that Jesus never wanted that in the first place (see Lk 10:38-42). If the spouse of a sex addict wants to be any good to her husband, she must take care of herself first. She will need to do three things:

1. *Break out of her caretaking role.* She needs to stop fixing, rescuing, saving, ministering to and "helping" everyone. She must see that she is doing it out of a need to be needed. If she were serving people the way they really needed to be served, she would let them carry more of their own responsibility (see Gal 6:5).

She must stop hiding from her own inadequacies behind a constant flurry of activity. She must stop blaming her husband for *her* feelings and choices and start taking responsibility for herself. After all, she has no power to change her husband; she has power to change only herself, and that only with God's help.

#2. *Let other people love her.* The codependent spouse likes to be the great benefactor to everyone else, but she hates to be on the receiving end. The fact is, as long as she is doing for everyone else, she can feel adequate and thereby protect herself from the deep sense of worthlessness that lurks within.

The healthiest thing she could do is to commit herself to a small group of women and say, "I need you. Can you love me and show me my blind spots?" She needs other women who will accept *her,* care for *her* and be there for *her* right where she is.

She needs true sisters in the Lord who will affirm her value and will love her enough to challenge her self-importance and gently confront her when she falls into old patterns.

#3. Let God fill the emptiness. This is the greatest area of confusion for the codependent spouse. She labors under the delusion that God requires perfect performance. Only then, in her mind, can she feel acceptable and worthwhile. She has a difficult time sitting at Jesus' feet and simply basking in his love. When she does pray or read the Bible, it becomes one more place to prove herself. She doesn't realize that God needs nothing from her and simply wants to give (Mt 11:28-30). When she is quiet before him, she doesn't always feel loved, because she is accustomed to winning the love of others. This is what she's had to do since she was a little girl, and it's hard for her to not apply the same "rules" to God.

She must learn the secret of letting her guard down and allowing Jesus Christ to touch her at her point of emptiness. When she does, she will begin to feel accepted and worthwhile for who she is, *apart from what she does.* From that place of security she can then begin serving others out of her fullness rather than her deficit. Because she will be in a place where she can freely receive from God, she will be able to give freely to others (Mt 10:8). The old, guilt-induced mentality will be replaced by a new freedom to live and love in a way closer to what God intended.

Conclusion
What is a wife to do? Grieve well, set boundaries and face herself. If she can let God and others love her back to wholeness, she will be the kind of wife that her husband needs. "Charm is deceptive, and beauty is fleeting; but a woman who fears the LORD is to be praised" (Prov 31:30).

Appendix B

The Twelve
Essentials

1. We must embrace Jesus Christ and the document that reveals his nature and directives—the Bible. Without this initial, basic step no genuine recovery is possible.

2. We must establish at least one to three supportive relationships for the purpose of accountability. Without this we will be deluded regarding our motives and unable to control our behavior.

3. We must courageously and honestly explore the dynamics of our original family. Otherwise, formative trauma will be hidden to us, and false self-concepts will remain intact.

4. We must understand how we responded to formative trauma and how that response is perpetuated today. Otherwise, we will remain stuck in self-defeating attitudes and behaviors, all the while blaming them on someone else.

5 We must explore the origins and content of our perceptions of God. Faulty thinking and responses must be corrected if we hope to develop

trust and experience reparenting.

6. We must uncover the false beliefs we have about ourselves and deliberately confront them, consistently, with the liberating truths of Scripture. Failure to do this results in psychological defeat and collusion with Satan.

7. We must grasp our fundamental brokenness and stop pretending we are something else.

8. We must understand and embrace the grace of God. Otherwise, we will never feel safe in our relationship with him, and we will not have the freedom to fail.

9. We must come to terms with our personal malevolence and stop assuming our own purity and infallibility.

10. We must differentiate between genuine emotional deprivation and the long-standing pattern of sin that obscures it, knowing where one ends and the other begins.

11. We must understand our sexual ritual and the underlying need it symbolizes, learning to meet God and others in this very place.

12. We must pursue the lifelong work of accountability and honesty in all our relationships and seek to model these values for others. This is evangelism in its truest form.

Appendix C

Further Reading

Insights into Sexual Addiction

Arterburn, Steve. *Addicted to "Love."* Ann Arbor, Mich.: Servant, 1991. An excellent resource for anyone drawn toward unhealthy relationships. It outlines the characteristics of sexual, relational and romance addictions.

Carnes, Patrick. *Out of the Shadows.* Center City, Minn.: Hazelden, 1992. The classic book on sex addiction and the core beliefs of the sex addict (secular).

Laaser, Mark R. *Faithful and True.* Grand Rapids, Mich.: Zondervan, 1996. A good book dealing with the cultural and family dynamics behind sex addiction. Outlines the twelve-step approach to healing.

Perkins, Bill. *Fatal Attractions.* Eugene, Ore.: Harvest House, 1991. A concise book showing that addictions often come in clusters (sex, food, work and so on). Gives clear guidelines for understanding addiction and the process of change.

Help for Spouses

Groom, Nancy. *From Bondage to Bonding.* Colorado Springs, Colo.: NavPress, 1991. An honest book on the subject of codependency. Provides clear biblical answers.

Hall, Laurie. *An Affair of the Mind.* Colorado Springs, Colo.: Focus on the Family, 1996. A powerful book written by the wife of a sex addict. It details how God led her to wholeness as she confronted her husband's sickness as well as her own.

Hemfelt, Robert, Frank Minirth and Paul Meier. *Love Is a Choice.* Nashville: Nelson, 1989. An outstanding resource for those wishing to understand codependency from a Christian perspective.

Christian Growth and Recovery

Cloud, Henry, and John Townsend. *Boundaries.* Grand Rapids, Mich.: Zondervan, 1992. A superb book dealing with our tendency to lose ourselves in others and then blame them when our life doesn't work out. Practical and biblical.

Cloud, Henry, and John Townsend. *False Assumptions.* Grand Rapids, Mich.: Zondervan, 1994. Exposes the lies that many well-meaning Christians believe about growth and recovery. Especially good for those who have a hard time reconciling Christianity with psychology.

Biblical Self-Image
McDowell, Josh. *Building Your Self-Image.* Wheaton, Ill.: Tyndale, 1984. A first-rate book dealing with the issue of self-esteem. It shows that the Bible has a great deal to say about this often misunderstood subject.

Wilson, Sandra D. *Released from Shame.* Downers Grove, Ill.: InterVarsity Press, 1990. Explores the whole issue of shame and offers powerful insights from Scripture. *Must* reading for every sex addict or spouse.

Healthy Sexuality
Hart, Archibald. *The Sexual Man.* Dallas: Word, 1994. An excellent resource for men or women wishing to understand the characteristics of normal male sexuality.

Penner, Clifford and Joyce. *The Gift of Sex.* Dallas: Word, 1981. *The* classic book on healthy married sexuality from a Christian perspective.

The Grace of God
Bridges, Jerry. *Transforming Grace.* Colorado Springs, Colo.: NavPress, 1991. In my opinion, the most balanced and biblically accurate book on the subject. A breath of fresh air for Christians (addicted or otherwise) who hunger for freedom from having to perform.

Manning, Brennan. *The Ragamuffin Gospel.* Sisters, Ore.: Multnomah, 1990. Shows how radical the grace of God really is. Excellent for those with "tilted halos," on the verge of giving up.

Healthy View of God
Tozer, A. W. *The Attributes of God.* Camp Hill, Penn.: Christian Publications, 1997. Tozer is a passionate and articulate writer. In this book he confronts the many misconceptions we have about God and presents a breathtaking and biblically accurate picture.

McClung, Floyd. *The Father Heart of God.* Eugene, Ore.: Harvest House, 1985. Excellent for those who have been neglected or hurt in the past and tend to struggle in their relationship with God as a result. Conveys the reality of God's compassion and love for broken people.

Appendix D

Resources for Additional Help

If you or someone you love struggles with sex addiction, it is imperative that you get all the support and help available. The following resources may be of assistance.

Exodus International—North America, P.O. Box 77652, Seattle, WA 98177. Phone: (206) 784-7799. Fax: (206) 784-7872. Homepage: http://exodus.base.org. Exodus International is a worldwide coalition of Christian ministries that offer support to men and women seeking to overcome homosexuality. In addition, many of these ministries offer support and resources to heterosexual sex addicts and their spouses. Contact them for a complete list of referral ministries in your area.

Fresno New Creation Ministries, P.O. Box 5451, Fresno, CA 93755. Phone: (559) 227-1066. Fax: (559) 227-4182. NCM does seminars and workshops around the U.S. on issues related to sex addiction, homosexuality and policy formation for churches and denominations. NCM staff offer telephone counseling and other resources. They also work in conjunction with a local in-patient facility that offers psychological and psychiatric services to Christians who are able to relocate for a short time.

American Family Association, Outreach Division, P.O. Drawer 2440, Tupelo, MS 38803. Phone: (601) 844-5128. E-mail: nclement@ebicom.net. Homepage: http://www.gocin.com/afa/or/outrch1.htm. AFA does workshops around the U.S. on issues related to sex addicts and their spouses. It also offers outstanding books, articles, tapes and telephone counseling. An excellent resource for those unable to find support in their area.

Christian Counseling

Individual and couples counseling is often a crucial part of the healing process. I recommend that counseling be pursued in conjunction with group support and accountability. Two organizations that can give you a referral to a Christian counselor in your area are:

Focus on the Family, 8605 Explorer Drive, Colorado Springs, CO 80920. Phone: (719) 531-3400, extension 2700.

Rapha, 5500 Interstate North Parkway, Suite 102, Atlanta, GA 30328. Phone: 1-800-383-HOPE.

Notes

Chapter 1: What We Are Dealing With
[1]Archibald Hart, *The Sexual Man* (Dallas: Word, 1994), p. 4.
[2]These are adapted from Mary M. Gergen, Jerry M. Suls, Ralph L. Rosnow and Robert E. Lana, *Psychology: A Beginning* (San Diego: Harcourt Brace Jovanovich, 1989), pp. 454-55.
[3]Hart, *The Sexual Man*, p. 52.
[4]Ibid., p. 53.
[5]Ibid., p. 89.

Chapter 2: The Dynamics of Sexual Addiction
[1]Stephen Arterburn, *Addicted to Love* (Ann Arbor, Mich.: Servant, 1991), pp. 80-85.
[2]For further reading on the neurological aspects of addiction, see Gerald May, *Addiction and Grace* (New York: Harper & Row, 1988), pp. 83-87.
[3]Jeffrey Satinover, *Homosexuality and the Politics of Truth* (Grand Rapids, Mich.: Baker, 1996), p. 134.
[4]Ibid., p. 136.
[5]Ibid., pp. 140-41.
[6]Gergen et al., *Psychology*, pp. 65-67.
[7]Patrick Carnes, *Out of the Shadows* (Center City, Minn.: Hazelden, 1992), p. 120.

Chapter 3: Where We Start
[1]Robert T. Michael, John H. Gagnon, Edward O. Laumann and Gina Kolata, *Sex in America: A Definitive Survey* (Boston: Little, Brown, 1994), p. 103.
[2]Ibid., p. 157.
[3]U.S. Bureau of the Census, 1984.
[4]This statement is from a study by Neil Malamuth and Edward Donnerstein in 1984. It is quoted in Curtis O. Byer and Louis W. Shainberg, *Dimensions of Human Sexuality*, 3rd ed. (Dubuque, Iowa: Wm. C. Brown, 1991), p. 561.
[5]This approach to Bible study was presented by Pastor Guy Greg of Riverwest Church in Portland, Oregon. He does not remember the original source.

Chapter 4: Enlisting the Help of Others
[1]Satinover, *Homosexuality and the Politics of Truth*, pp. 141-43.
[2]Much research indicates, and my own counseling experience confirms, that a root issue for men who struggle with homosexual desires is an unmet need for same-sex love carried over from childhood. The pathway to healing therefore would not involve *avoidance* of the same sex but active *involvement* with healthy heterosexual males. For further reading that elaborates on this concept I recommend Bob Davies and Lori Rentzel, *Coming Out of Homosexuality* (Downers Grove, Ill.: InterVarsity Press, 1993); Joe Dallas, *Desires in Conflict* (Eugene, Ore.: Harvest House, 1991); Joseph Nicolosi, *Reparative Therapy of Male Homosexuality* (New York: Jason Aronson, 1991); Elizabeth Moberly, *Homosexuality: A New Christian Ethic* (Greenwood, S.C.: Attic Press, 1983).

Chapter 7: The Divine Caricature

[1]God's love for you is forever settled in Scripture. If you tend to judge your lovableness based on how you feel at any given time, you might do well to meditate on these clear statements: Isaiah 54:10; Jeremiah 31:3; Hosea 14:4; Zephaniah 3:17; Romans 8:38-39; Ephesians 2:4-5; 2 Timothy 1:7; 1 John 4:16, 18-19; Jude 21.

Chapter 10: The Unexpected Response

[1]See 1 Kings 21:20-29, where God shows mercy to Ahab, the most wicked king in Israel's history. See also Nahum 1—3, which describes Nineveh's wickedness, then Jonah 1—4, which details their repentance and subsequent forgiveness.

Chapter 12: The Hunt of the Malnourished Heart

[1]This quote comes from a book I read years ago. I regret that I cannot give the author credit since I cannot track the source.